Ditching the Doormat

Identifying and Recovering From
Dysfunctional Relationships and
Marriages, Setting New Boundaries, and
Reclaiming the Life You Want

A Doormat Series Book

Alexis Carter, MA

<u>The Doormat Series of Self-Help Books and Workbooks</u>

<u>by Alexis Carter</u>

Stop Being a Doormat and Learn to Love Yourself

Ditching the Doormat

Leave That Junk Behind- A Self-Esteem Workbook for Adults

You've Got This Girl- A Self-Esteem Workbook for Girls

Table of Contents

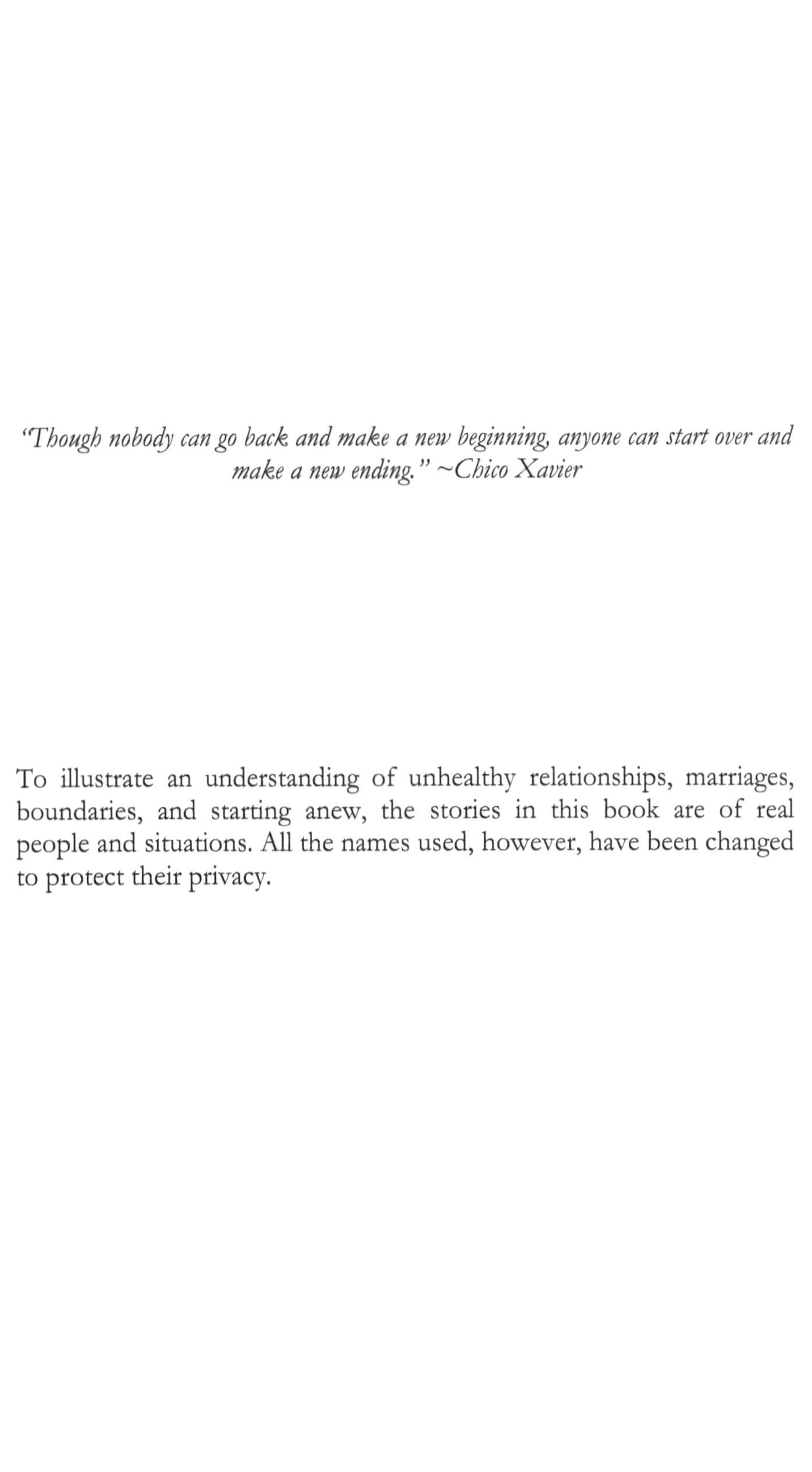

"Though nobody can go back and make a new beginning, anyone can start over and make a new ending." ~Chico Xavier

To illustrate an understanding of unhealthy relationships, marriages, boundaries, and starting anew, the stories in this book are of real people and situations. All the names used, however, have been changed to protect their privacy.

Introduction

We will find ourselves in a challenging or troubled relationship at some point in life. It might be within our family, friendship, work, or marriage. We might not recognize how unhealthy it is, and we convince ourselves that we are happy and that it is normal. We may know something is wrong but feel stuck, unsure, or scared to move on. Or, we might have decided to end the relationship or marriage and are trying to figure out how to create a new life for ourselves.

You may be disheartened at the thought of closing an old chapter of your life to start afresh, worry about what other people say, or agonize over being alone. Recovering from committed relationships is a lengthy process that takes time and effort. No one expects you to stand up and forget all the effort you put into your relationship at once, but there is more to enjoy past the toxicity and emotional turmoil.

A dysfunctional marriage or relationship is not the end or failure. Every negative experience, trauma, or unplanned life event is something to learn from with wisdom and confidence. *Ditching The Doormat* is for men and women suffering from or recovering from divorce and dysfunctional relationships. It provides insight into learned behavioral patterns and provides practical and sometimes humorous advice for gaining confidence, building self-esteem, and eliminating repeated unwanted behaviors that keep us in a rut. Doing so allows you to set new, healthy boundaries and reclaim the life you want.

A toxic relationship can make you feel helpless and miserable. You start to feel negative about your life, and your self-confidence may plummet. Not all relationships start stormy; some become worse over time. I have never met anyone who, at the beginning of a relationship or marriage, said, "I DO, and I hope our relationship becomes an emotional nightmare." We will discuss what makes good relationships turn sour and when to know when it's time to let go.

I can think of at least two personal relationships in my life that I look back on and shake my head. Why and how did I ever stay in that toxic relationship? How could I have tolerated such unhealthy behavior while teaching others to do the opposite? With hindsight, I can see how I temporarily lost part of myself. You are not alone here; we all have fallen prey to accommodating negative behavior to avoid further heartache, financial stress, and being alone. I will provide many examples, along with my learned life lessons, to demonstrate that we are all human, we make errors, and the key is to learn from them.,

In my book, *Stop Being a Doormat and Learn to Love Yourself,* I review the origins of doormat behavior and thinking. I go into greater detail on codependency and how to recognize the traits and develop skills for self-love. When I wrote it, I wanted to expand on toxic relationships and provide practical advice on identifying them, ending them, and moving forward confidently. Hence, this book quickly developed as a topic of its own.

This book is written for men and women in different stages of unhealthy relationships and marriages. You may be in the middle of a dysfunctional relationship and are contemplating moving forward without them, but you need the skills to do so. Or perhaps you are newly single and want to learn how to avoid repeating problems in the next relationship. You may need to re-establish healthy boundaries with people and restore self-confidence. Recovering from toxic relationships and lifeless marriages is challenging but doable. You can do this, and you will develop the skills to take charge and claim the life you want.

Let's get started!

Chapter 1:

What is a Toxic, Doormat Relationship?

"Let your hopes, not your hurts, shape your future." ~*Robert H. Schuller*

A doormat allows others to walk all over them. They either never, or eventually, after years of unhappiness, say, "ENOUGH!". They tolerate what is intolerable to others and do not demand more for themselves. They may be codependent on others. They may have low self-esteem. They may have such low self-confidence from challenging life experiences that they have never been encouraged to love themselves and expect more out of life.

Sometimes we hold on to relationships so hard that we may not notice something is out of place. Some feel stuck in a relationship that they know isn't healthy but don't know what is wrong with it. Others have left an unhealthy relationship or marriage and are concerned they will keep dating the same type of person in the next chapter of their lives. Your first step toward ditching the doormat and moving on is recognizing your relationship patterns.

Think of someone you know struggling with self-confidence and repeated toxic relationships.

- Do they rely on others to make them feel happy and fulfilled?

- Do they need reassurance and validation that they are pretty, smart, or capable?

- Do they tolerate abusive, disrespectful, or miserable partners because it is easier than starting over?

- Do they blame themselves for the problems in the relationship?

- Do they avoid conflict out of fear of being alone?

- Do any of these examples apply to you?

I knew a kind woman named Lisa who, with good intentions, allowed her life to be completely engulfed in that of her husband and children. After an unstable, neglected childhood and driven by desperation for stability, Lisa was driven to cherish her family through ups and downs.

Lisa and her husband, Marc, had two children, and she did everything possible to keep her home, children, and Marc happy. She avoided conflict, bent over backward to be at three places at once to accommodate each member, and quit her job as a nurse to be available 24/7 to her family. She never complained and never prioritized herself.

Marc was controlling and narcissistic, often withholding affection or gratitude until he got what he wanted from Lisa. Additionally, he had an affair with a co-worker and would openly call and text her in front of Lisa. Lisa had no personal sense of identity and allowed her husband to be disrespectful and humiliate her to live the dream she had of a perfect family.

Lisa knew Marc was disrespectful and cruel but told herself that a divorce would be too traumatic for her children. She also worried about financially supporting herself if she left Marc. When I met Lisa, she told me it was her duty as a mother to provide a stable and loving home for her children, and her needs and wants didn't matter while her family relied on her.

She held on to her marriage for two additional years and genuinely didn't feel she deserved any better. She doubled down on her efforts to please Marc, underwent plastic surgery, and lost 20 lbs. to appear more appealing. While noble, sacrificing her mental health and happiness for her children, Lisa could not appreciate the unhealthy dynamics her children were witnessing. Eventually, with therapy and self-care, Lisa decided to leave the marriage. She worked on developing self-confidence and establishing a new life outside her children and emotionally abusive husband. Eventually, she found great pride and satisfaction from her inner strength and fortitude.

Many of you might feel that Lisa's behavior is extreme and that her psychological issues result from deeply rooted childhood traumas. You are correct to an extent. Our environments and experiences growing up significantly affect how we think and behave as adults. However, they are not a blueprint written in stone. It is possible to "un-learn" unhealthy behavioral patterns from childhood, be self-confident, and thrive as an adult. Lisa's behavior and emotional needs are present to some degree in all unhealthy doormat relationships.

Doormat Dynamics in Relationships

Most of us have a hundred excuses to ignore hints and red flags that our relationship is unhealthy. This passive avoidance of problems only leads to dysfunction and encourages the same behavior to repeat in the next relationship. It is critical to be aware of unhealthy relationship patterns to stop the cycle and start anew. You are reading this book to make significant, positive changes to your life and improve your self-worth. Having insight into what unhealthy behavioral patterns exist for you, learning to stop them from repeating, and replacing them with positive habits is critical to this process.

Perhaps you are similar to Lisa, who, desperate to create the life she never had, actively chose to ignore unacceptable behavior and tolerated being treated as a doormat to avoid uprooting the life she wanted. Maybe you have different codependent traits that cause you to fear conflict. Some might decide to keep their relationship going for fear of disapproval by others; others may worry more about how they would carry on if they separated—financially or emotionally.

In every relationship, there will be ups and downs. Staying tuned into your values, needs, and self-worth is critical to weathering this rollercoaster. Ignoring the warning signs, and allowing doormat mentalities to prevail, can lead to a slow, painful deterioration of your relationships, self-confidence, self-esteem, and happiness.

Blame and Destructive Criticism

Blame and criticism will destroy a relationship because they create a hostile, unbalanced dynamic in which one person is blamed or criticized by the other. This will invariably lead to resentment and distance between the two of you. Constant criticism and a lack of positive reinforcement can and will destroy your relationship when it becomes a pattern.

When criticism becomes incorporated into your daily life, it paves the way for more negativity, including a lack of communication and replacing love for your partner with anger and frustration, leading to more destructive relationship habits like emotional abuse. You and your partner can fall into a cyclical pattern in which the problem reoccurs with increasing frequency and severity. This will lead to withdrawing from one another, and you or your partner will start experiencing feelings of lonesomeness.

It is unrealistic to expect two completely different humans never to experience conflict. However, there is a significant distinction between a complaint and destructive criticism. A statement that is not specific and that expresses negative feelings or opinions about the personality or character of your partner is called criticism.

If your partner has habits or behaviors that annoy or bother you, you might complain to them. For example, a common complaint between men and women is that men leave the toilet seat up. If you ask him not to and repeatedly complain to him when the behavior continues, the complaints may intensify. After some time, you may blame him and shift your attention to criticizing his character rather than his actions. If you continue to harbor anger toward your partner, you may create a negative narrative about that connection. You may start keeping a tally of your partner's mistakes, which can make it difficult for you to recognize the positive aspects.

John and Kayla had been in a relationship for one year. Recently, Kayla began to tell John that his clothing was out of fashion and that he needed to improve the interior design of his home. John took great pride in his home and was hurt that Kayla didn't like his décor choices, but he never conveyed his feelings to Kayla. Kayla, who was not aware she was overly critical and hurtful, continued to point out changes he should make to his persona, home, and career choices to "help better him." Over the next year, John grew to feel diminished, insecure, and unhappy. Kayla eventually broke up with John, saying she no longer respected him. In turn, John blamed Kayla for the demise of their relationship without ever recognizing his role in their destructive communication patterns.

Lack of Intimacy and Communication

When you first met your partner, you hopefully had an intense physical and emotional attraction for them. You probably also communicated well and respected the other's opinions and needs. Lack of intimacy and communication may never have crossed your mind as a possibility in the future.

In 2008, a sample of 886 divorced individuals in Hennepin County, Minnesota, took a survey on what led to their divorce. Growing apart and being unable to communicate well were the two most often cited reasons for getting a divorce—55% and 53%, respectively (Hawkins et al., 2012).

When there is a lack of emotional connection between two people, there is a lack of intimacy, which will strain the relationship. It's not only about being physically close to one another but also about the intangibles, such as communication, comprehension, and trust. Without these qualities, a romantic connection will become stale and unsatisfying. As you move forward from unhealthy relationships into new ones, it is essential to be mindful of these qualities that need to be present for a connection to survive.

Maria and Peter have been married for 15 years and have three children under the age of 18 at home. They started out their marriage with the hopes and dreams that we all have when we think we have found "The One." The first few years were happy, with normal ups and downs but they still had fun with each other, were respectful and kind, and had a wonderful sex life. After they had their first child, their sex life started to wane. Both were exhausted and stressed from being new parents and before they knew it, they had two more children added to the mix.

Both Peter and Maria had full-time jobs in addition to their roles as parents. They were loving, doting parents who were highly involved in their children's lives- attending soccer and baseball games multiple times a week, ballet classes, school volunteering, swimming… you name it. They were running ragged from the afterschool responsibilities and parenting duties and fell into a routine of waking, getting the kids out the door, working, picking the kids up, running all over town, feeding, bathing, and sleeping. They didn't make a conscious effort to create time for themselves, even a five-minute check-in to make sure the other was okay and to remind themselves that they loved one another. They had fallen into a routine of parenting and cohabitating and lost their roles as partners. Their intimacy was all but non-existent and would go months without having sex.

By the time they reached the 15-year mark of their marriage, both Mary and Peter were seeking marriage counseling as they felt they had lost their passion for the marriage and didn't know how to reconnect with each other. Mary told me she felt like she was a roommate that happened to share a bed with her roommate. She felt unattractive and ignored. Peter also felt lonely and disconnected from Mary. Neither one recognized that they had forgotten each other, had forgotten to nurture their relationship, and had fallen into a "Friend Zone."

This is an incredibly common issue with marriage after kids or other years of relationship neglect. It is absolutely possible to recover from this pattern once you both recognize the issues and actively work to remedy them.

Below are common red flags associated with poor emotional connection and lack of intimacy :

- **Distance between the two of you**: As the level of emotional closeness in a relationship wanes, one standard coping and self-protection measure is emotionally distancing oneself and withdrawing from the other person.

- **You feel lonely**: Loneliness is one of the most excruciating experiences in a marriage; you spend so much time with your partner and still feel alone. You share life, sleep in the same room, and yet feel like you don't know them. Suppose you and your spouse share a home but still experience isolation, miscommunication, or distance. In that case, this is an unmistakable sign that there is a significant problem with the emotional connection in your relationship.

- **You are less affectionate**: A romantic connection that lacks emotional intimacy risks deteriorating into one that lacks affection. A relationship with little to no sexual activity is generally always indicative of a lack of emotional connection. Living with a partner, sharing a home, paying bills, and raising children without a physical and intimate relationship is bound to be a struggle.

Lack of Respect

A happy, mutually respectful partnership is one of the essential elements we think of when we envision our future with a partner. This entails someone who respects and cares about their partner and stops to consider how their actions may affect them. Respect is a mandatory element to successful relationships. If you feel this doesn't exist in your relationship, I encourage you to consider how you got to that point.

Roger and Michelle had been partners for five years. Their relationship was based on love, respect, and commonalities that kept their lives fulfilled and balanced. When Roger was laid off from his job as an architect, he struggled to find new work. He was also depressed that his career had come to a grinding halt and found himself sleeping most days and was totally unmotivated to find a new job.

Michelle felt really bad for Roger and tried to be as supportive as she knew how. She let him sleep and avoid job searching for a couple of weeks before she started to wonder if he was going to try to find a job again. Her work as a dentist paid well, but they had a lifestyle, mortgage, and financial responsibilities that required two incomes to live comfortably. Michelle gently brought this to Roger's attention that it was time to get back out there and find another job. She even offered to move her practice to a new city if she had to. Michelle felt that Roger didn't recognize her efforts to encourage and support him which caused her to feel resentful and angry. These feelings built and built over several weeks as Roger made almost no progress with finding a new job. He seemed content to be a house-husband and showed no interest in going back to work. He also avoided talking to Michelle because he felt depressed and ashamed that he wasn't helping to support them.

Michelle grew so frustrated and angry at Roger's lack of motivation and ambition that she began to lose respect for him. She was embarrassed to tell people that he didn't want to find a job and felt that it reflected on her as a person. She lost all interest in sex and intimacy and generally avoided Roger's touch. At angry moments, she lashed out, telling him he wasn't acting like a "real man" since he couldn't take care of his responsibilities and wanted to live like a child, totally dependent on her.

Their lack of mutual respect for each other's needs, their significant communication breakdown, and lack of intimacy started to drive a significant wedge between them that neither felt was recoverable.

The following are warning indications that your partner does not respect you.

- **Being constantly embarrassed by your partner**: It is common to have playful banter in happy relationships. When you let your partner poke a little fun at you with harmless jokes, you know that they won't take it too far. It is a sign of mutual trust between you. However, this trust disappears when your partner deliberately tries to humiliate or embarrass you, perhaps by making fun of you in front of friends, publicizing your secrets, or degrading you on social media. Passive aggressive teasing only decreases self-esteem and has no place in a positive partnership.

- **Not taking the time to address your concerns**: If you are not satisfied with how your partner leaves the kitchen sink dirty, proper communication allows a productive dialogue about how to solve this. Not expressing your needs and concerns will only cause them to fester until they reappear in a much more destructive way.

- **Your achievements and qualities are ignored**: Every person on this planet possesses a one-of-a-kind collection of qualities and achievements, each of which they have every right to be proud of. One of the most critical responsibilities of partners is to support and encourage each other. Refusing to acknowledge somebody's qualities or accomplishments is a display of disrespect.

Secret Keeping

Recent studies have shown that infidelity, money troubles, and substance abuse are the most damaging secrets kept by couples.

Researchers have determined that adultery accounts for between 20%–40% of all divorces in the United States (Marín et al., 2014).

Secrets foster a sense of mistrust which can grow exponentially with the slightest hint of deception. Think of the analogy, "One step forward and two steps back." Trying to regain trust is more like "One tiny shuffle forward and ten giant leaps back" after any hint of new betrayals.

Loss of trust leaves the foundation of the relationship as a whole vulnerable to manipulation. Earning and maintaining trust is integral for a relationship to survive. If it doesn't exist for you, you need to consider if it is possible to recover from it.

In the next chapter, we will continue identifying a toxic relationship and examine the characteristics of destructive, doormat relationships. As you read it, be mindful of your relationships, past and present, and honestly evaluate if the elements resonate with you. The goal is to identify unwanted, harmful behavioral patterns you don't want to replicate as you move forward.

Chapter 2:

Is My Relationship Toxic?

Courage isn't having the strength to go on – it's going on when you don't have strength." -napoleon bonaparte.

Deciding to end a serious relationship or marriage is a significant decision. Some might assume that any relationship which ends could be considered toxic, or else it would have been successful. I am reluctant to agree with this because I have met several people who have separated or divorced and stayed close friends, some even best friends. They felt they were incompatible as partners but loved and valued each other as friends.

> Michael and Emily had been best friends since the age of 12. Their close friendship eventually led to a romantic relationship, and they were married at age 18. One year later, they had a baby and struggled to make ends meet. They moved in with her parents, and soon, the combination of immaturity, financial strain, lack of personal time, and the stress of being new parents did not bode well for the success of their marriage. They divorced at age 21 but remained close friends and excellent co-parents and even attended each other's weddings five years later. It would be a happy world if every relationship could end like this, but this example is most likely in the minority of divorces.

Every relationship has different strengths and weaknesses, and you both will have good and bad days. Specific values and elements must be present to nurture and grow a healthy relationship. When they are not, the building blocks of toxicity and dysfunction begin to grow and fester.

Consider where you are at in your life now. Are you trying to make a rocky relationship work? Looking for a way out of a dysfunctional one?

Trying to understand what led to the end of your marriage? Or are you ready to rebuild, set boundaries, cultivate new, healthier relationships, and just not sure what to look for? Ask yourself the following questions:

- Does your partner provide support, love, and understanding?

- Do you both work together to maintain positive and constructive communication?

- Do you feel emotionally and physically safe in your relationship?

- Do you feel uplifted when you are with your partner?

- Do you bring out the best in each other?

- Do you have a solid base of respect for each other?

- Do you feel unsupported in your relationship?

- Have you ever lost your sense of self due to your or your partner's codependency?

- Does your partner gaslight you and blame you for their issues?

- Do you feel misunderstood and insecure about the stability of the relationship?

- Are you ever degraded and made to doubt your worth?

- Is your emotional, psychological, or physical well-being ever in jeopardy?

Now review what you answered yes and no to. Did any ring true more than others, and why? As you transition from dysfunctional, unhealthy relationships into the kind you deserve, keep these questions in mind about what you want and don't want in a new partner.

At its most fundamental level, a relationship can become toxic over time if it consistently contributes to a person feeling worse rather than better. Relationships harmful to your health can form in virtually any environment between any individual, gender, or age.

Effects of Toxic Relationships

The effects of a toxic relationship can be severe and far-reaching. They can cause low self-esteem, anxiety, depression, and physical harm. Toxic relationships can also have adverse effects on the relationships around you.

It's crucial to recognize the signs of a toxic relationship and to seek help if you are in one. This may involve you seeking support from friends and family, therapy or counseling, or sometimes, leaving the relationship. It is also essential to understand that toxic behavior is not always easy to identify, and there is no shame in asking for help.

It's difficult to leave a toxic relationship because we usually keep hoping it will improve with enough time, love, and energy. This generally does not happen. You need to love and respect yourself and realize you deserve better.

Characteristics and Signs of a Toxic Relationship

Do you remember the movie *Grease*? Sandy and Danny spend most of the movie dancing and singing around town about how much they love each other. Still, they never seem to come together until they both decide to transform their appearance, attitude, sex appeal, and hobbies to be attractive to the other. They then fall in love with the "new and improved" version of themselves; everyone sings and frolics around some more, and they literally fly off into the sunset, happily ever after.

Or an even better one, *Fatal Attraction,* which should be called: "Tips You Might Be Dating a Stalker." Here Michael Douglas keeps returning to his mistress, Glenn Close, enjoying the attention, sex, and admiration while painfully oblivious to the codependent, crazy, bunny-murdering behavior. Likewise, instead of saying, "I'm out!" when Michael Douglas makes it clear he doesn't want a real relationship with her, only sex, Glenn Close keeps at it like a doormat, pleads for him to come back, and it ultimately leads to a bloody ending.

These popular movies depicted extraordinarily toxic relationships in an entertaining Hollywood way. However, toxic relationships are sometimes harder to identify and are never entertaining. They can be incredibly painful, and heart-wrenching, and affect our physical and mental health. While there are obvious signs like verbal, psychological, and physical abuse, there are more subtle cues that we often choose to overlook or decide are "not that bad."

All relationships have some toxicity; we are different people coming together in close quarters and sharing life's most significant emotional, financial, and familial stressors for years. Naturally, there will be some give and take and imbalance at times. However, a healthy relationship will right itself with awareness of this imbalance and work to be respectful and cognizant of the other's needs. <u>No one</u> is a doormat for long in a healthy relationship.

When toxicity passes the tipping point, you will always be aware of it at some level.

- You are uneasy and frustrated.
- You feel insecure about the relationship.
- You sense red flags but can't quite figure out what they are.
- You start doubting your future together.
- You feel you are trying and trying to make things work, but nothing ever does.
- You feel worse about yourself when you are together and happier when apart.

Below is a list of several red flags to help determine if your relationship or your history of relationships is toxic. If any of these resonate with you, it's time to get out and stop giving bits and pieces of your self-esteem away. You are worth more than that and deserve the best, not a sliver of the best.

- **There is a lack of emotional support.**

  A healthy relationship involves being there for each other during good and challenging times. In a toxic relationship, your partner may not provide emotional support, mock you, or minimize your feelings when you need his help.

- **Your partner is a gaslighter.**

  Gaslighting is a manipulative tactic your partner may use that causes you to doubt your perceptions or memories. They may deny things you know happened and use emotional manipulation to convince you that you are overreacting or imagining things. This can lead to feelings of confusion and insecurity.

- **You have become increasingly isolated.**

  When someone tries to limit your social activities and personal relationships or discourage you from spending time with loved ones, you can feel isolated, lonely, and insecure, which leads to a feeling of loss of control in your life.

- **There is unhealthy communication.**

  Healthy communication is the cornerstone of any stable relationship. Whether it be at home, with friends, or at work, constructive and healthy communication fosters trust, stability, and mutual respect. In a toxic relationship, communication may be abusive, disrespectful, or one-sided. You may feel like you cannot express your thoughts and feelings or that your opinions are not valued.

- **You feel insecure all the time.**

  Healthy relationships bring out the best in us. They don't cause us to doubt our self-worth and value. You both positively reinforce your feelings and mutual support through physical and verbal acts of kindness. If you are in a constant state of insecurity, you are in a dysfunctional relationship.

- **Your partner constantly criticizes you.**

  Partners support; they don't pick at one another. Criticism will invariably cause one of you to feel insecure and uncertain about yourself or where you stand in the relationship. In a healthy relationship, partners listen to each other's opinions; even if they disagree, they respect each other's individuality. Giving unsolicited, passive-aggressive advice on improving something you are doing or pointing out flaws in your appearance is never acceptable. It is a sure sign that they do not respect or value you and you are in a toxic, doormat relationship.

- **You don't trust them.**

  Giving over total trust to a significant other can be difficult at first and may leave you feeling vulnerable. Trust takes time to build and strengthen as you get to know each other. Our family, best friends, and significant others are people with whom our trust should never be questioned. You should always feel they have your back, unconditionally support you, and will never betray you. It is a primary tenant in a relationship that should never be overlooked if lost or damaged.

- **Your partner likes to play games, and you keep losing at them.**

Game playing must be one of the most frustrating behaviors in courtships and relationships. Sometimes it is to test the waters and see how serious someone is. Or it could be to see how far they can go before you ask for more. Or even worse, they only show interest in you and your relationship after you start to pull away. Whatever the game, if you are an unhappy player or find yourself in your own *Squid Games*, it is time to throw in the dice and move on.

In healthy relationships, you can depend on your partner. When they say they love you, they don't tell you that they aren't sure about you the next day. You can rely on them to follow through, not cause you to worry, wonder if they will show up, or text.

Game players are not serious about your relationship. They are focused on themselves and their needs. Manipulating you is simply part of their narcissistic display of insecurity. You don't need this, and you should never be a doormat to a game player.

- **They chip away at your self-esteem and confidence.**

Toxic relationships are destroyers of healthy self-esteem. Think of them as terminators, slowly walking through your mind and blasting away at your walls of confidence and self-worth. Through inconsistent affection, critical remarks about how you dress, look, or parent, or comments that make you feel dumb or worthless, you start to feel bad about yourself. You begin to *believe* these comments on some level.

Who was once a radiant individual full of self-assurance, optimism, and confidence, slowly becomes doubting, insecure, codependent, and depressed. If an evening with your partner makes you feel like this, it is time to get the @#$!$ out. This is not okay. This is not a relationship to stay in.

- **You keep waiting for them to change and believe you are the one to make it happen.**

Relationships are a two-way street. There are two of you that make it work or don't make it work. In a toxic relationship, one or both partners exhibit harmful behaviors while the other takes on the role of a doormat, allowing the behavior to continue.

A healthy relationship would never allow these toxic behaviors to continue. It would be a one-and-done situation where the healthy, confident, non-doormat recognizes they deserve better. There are no second, third, or fourth chances.

Sticking around and hoping your partner will "just work through their feelings" will only lead to heartbreak. My favorite doormat statement that I have heard from many men and women is, "If I love them enough, they might change."

Doormats hold on to hope of the relationship they have always dreamed of; they create a false image of their significant other in their minds and often lose sight of what is right in front of their face. Unless your partner is two years old and learning how to navigate the world and not bite their friends, you will not change them. Move on and find a mature person with the characteristics, values, and personality that is right for you. They are out there!

- **You feel worse when you are around them.**

In a healthy relationship, you are generally happy and satisfied to be with each other. When you are apart, you look forward to seeing them. But when you go over to your boyfriend's house, or when your wife arrives home from work and your stress level increases, your mood worsens, you feel bad about yourself, or you want to avoid them, then you are in a toxic relationship. If your partner doesn't help bring out the best in you, it's time to look closely at your relationship patterns.

- **You abandon self-care and your own needs.**

Being part of a couple can be a wonderful thing. It can provide fulfillment emotionally, mentally, and physically. But…it shouldn't be all your life is about. You need to make sure your individual needs are met too. Neglecting yourself, self-care and personal happiness can be as destructive as only focusing on your partner.

This must stop if you seem to always cater to your significant other's needs and ensure they are happy and satisfied first. Make sure you keep developing and growing your sense of self, independence, hobbies, and friends as you mature as a couple. The goal is to be as well-rounded and balanced as possible in a relationship, and focusing on just one of you leaves the other in a doormat role.

- **There is an imbalance of responsibilities.**

A relationship is a balance; like a seesaw, healthy partners will go up for you when the other is down and vice versa. You help each other and meet each other's needs. You can take and deliver feedback and constructive criticism without World War III starting.

If you find that you are always the one who does all the chores, all the planning, all the finances, and all the child-rearing, this is a sign of a toxic relationship. It is also a clear sign of codependent behaviors, which you are both enabling.

- **You are not the person you want to be when you are around them.**

Think of a time when you felt like your best self. Who were you around? What was happening in your life? What was contributing to your powerful self-confidence and positive self-esteem?

Take a look at the relationship you are re-evaluating now. Why is that best self not there? Why are you not the person you want to be?

When we are in a toxic relationship, we have poor self-confidence and self-esteem, have lost that pep we once had, second-guess our decisions, and are preoccupied with worrying that the relationship might end. If you were once a strong, confident, secure person, it should only get better in the right relationship, not worse.

- **Your mental health is shaky.**

I wish I could give you a magic tool to ensure you never have moments of anxiety, depression, or mental exhaustion. These moments will happen to all of us in life, and it is through life experiences, support, and self-awareness that we overcome them. If your relationship leaves you feeling exhausted and mentally drained, then a few problems are happening here. Not only are you involved with a toxic individual, but you are allowing yourself to stay there.

Ask yourself why? Why is your mental and physical health not a top priority for you? Why are you allowing someone to drain your life force? It is time to put yourself first, and then, you can find the healthy relationship you deserve.

- **You make excuses for them to friends and family.**

When you are in a relationship, being protective of your partner is normal and expected. However, when you protect them by making excuses for their insensitive, cruel, selfish, or unsupportive behavior, you are not protecting them- you are enabling them and keeping the behavior going.

Our friends and family love us and want us to be happy. Of course, you will be embarrassed when your boyfriend forgets your birthday, is late to your brother's wedding, teases you in front of friends, drinks too much, and passes out at a family dinner. If you make excuses to your family for your significant other's behavior, you are telling them, and yourself, that it isn't a problem. It is okay to be disrespected.

- **Your partner is too controlling or needy.**

If you find that your significant other tends to dominate the communication dynamics in the relationship, expects you to do what they want, and doesn't allow you to make decisions or have personal time, you are in an unhealthy, controlling relationship.

Is your partner worried you are cheating on them? Do they ask who you have been with when you go out with friends? Do they question whom you are texting? When you complain about their behavior, do they gaslight you and make you feel bad by saying it is just because they love you and you must not love them as much?

These are all signs of insecurity and fear, which do not equate with healthy relationships. Not addressed quickly and decisively, this behavior will lead to more problematic behaviors, such as various forms of abuse. This is not a person you want to be involved with. It can be exhausting to reassure someone constantly, and it is not your job.

- **Your relationship is teetering on the edge of abuse.**

There is a very short step between toxic, unwanted behaviors and abuse. Often, you are experiencing abuse, but because you aren't being beaten black and blue, you don't register it as harmful or abusive, and it can quickly become the norm in your relationship.

Verbal, psychological, and physical abuse are all insidious behaviors and exceptionally harmful to your mental and physical health. They are never, ever, to be tolerated. One emotional blackmail, one demeaning name-calling, and one push are all hard stops in a relationship. This is a critical dysfunctional relationship topic which we will delve further into in Chapter 4.

The longer you stay in a toxic relationship, the longer you tolerate and excuse behaviors that individuals in healthy relationships would find intolerable. Recognizing and removing yourself from them is more challenging the longer you stay. No one deserves to feel less than others, question their self-worth, or feel used and unimportant. You are a fantastic person, and it's time to expect more from yourself.

Several characteristics and behaviors create, enable, and perpetuate dysfunctional relationships. Many build upon each other and may be closely tied to learned patterns of behaviors from childhood, personality disorders, or mental health instability. Below, we will review four areas I have found to be consistently present in toxic, dysfunctional relationships and should be actively avoided in future relationships.

Hostile Communication

Any communication expressed in a manner that is disrespectful, abusive, or hurtful is an example of toxic, hostile communication. This can grow over time; often, you or your partner may not be aware that you are engaging in unhealthy patterns of communication with one another. It is common for one or both of you to be unwilling or unsure of how to eliminate the behavior. Below are examples of hostile communication that cause a destructive, cyclical effect of additional, unintended problems.

- **Contempt:** Contempt is comparable to criticism but much more destructive. It is typically an attempt to belittle or demean the other person and communicates disrespect and even disgust toward the individual being insulted. It may signify unexpressed negative feelings that slowly become ingrained in the relationship. Contempt can take the form of hurtful sarcasm, verbal hostility, ignoring, and eye-rolling.

- **Projection:** When a person experiences overwhelming negative emotions but believes those emotions belong to another person, they engage in projection. For example, if your partner is depressed about their job performance, they will project that insecurity and sadness onto you, and you may begin to feel depressed or moody. This occurs unintentionally most of the time and results in you adopting the emotional state of your spouse.

- **Assumptions:** Assuming your partner knows what you need or think without you telling them is a common problem. This often results in anger, frustration, and a perception that the other is oblivious to their needs.

- **Defensiveness:** It is only natural to feel the need to defend oneself if you have been on the receiving end of someone else's scorn. However, if defensiveness is used as a continuous communication tactic inside a marriage, it may harm the relationship. Being belittled or demeaned can cause someone to be defensive and lash out.

- **Blame-shifting:** If you or your partner are struggling with guilt in your relationship, one of you will use blame-shifting to give away your misery and take the focus off of yourself. You can free yourself from your anguish and shame if you successfully make your partner feel bad for what they have done. To shift responsibility, your partner may play mental games, reject responsibilities, tell lies, and twist the truth.

- **Victimhood:** A person who views themselves as a victim in a relationship will interpret every event as a deliberate attempt to cause them harm. When your partner is overly sensitive to everything you do, this could make you feel suffocated, and you might question if your partner ever considers your feelings. A victim mentality partner may do the following:

  - criticize you before you get a chance to tell them your concerns

  - act irrationally out of fear that you are about to leave them

  - act aggressively if they believe you are about to disagree with them

  - inappropriately react when questioned about anything they have done

The feelings of one party are the driving force behind the connection. They will use any means necessary, including manipulation and control, to coerce you into satisfying their profound need for love, safety, and security.

- **Hypersensitivity:** If your partner takes offense to everything, it might make you feel like you are constantly walking on ice. This is a form of codependency as they try to coerce you into making them feel better and taking care of them. If you do so and repeatedly enable unwanted behavior, you are possibly experiencing codependency issues as well.

Substance Abuse

Addiction to substances can harm all aspects of your or your partner's personal lives, including your relationships. It is highly toxic behavior in a relationship, and if this is an issue for you, your concerns about the status of your relationship are valid and essential to come to terms with. When your partner is addicted to a substance, they are often preoccupied with thoughts of the substance. Family, friends, and loved ones become secondary to their addiction. Below are just some areas in which this negatively impacts a relationship.

Loss of Trust

A healthy relationship must have trust as one of its foundational pillars. Abuse of drugs frequently results in broken trust. It is not unusual for someone who is addicted to drugs to engage in conduct that is secretive and to lie about their drug use. Your partner may lie about who they were with or what they were doing that day. They may even take or steal money from you to purchase substances. When your spouse lies, steals, or is dishonest, you can feel hurt, uncared for, and disrespected. The pressure that this can bring to any relationship is profound.

Financial Impact

Maintaining an active addiction comes at a high financial cost. Your partner may spend a substantial amount of money on supporting their addiction. They might not be able to keep consistent work, so they rely on others for financial aid. When your inhibitions are lower, you have diminished impulse control, and high-risk behaviors and spending frequently occur.

Employment and Education

Depending on the severity of the addiction, employment, and education can also be negatively impacted in numerous ways. Partners who indulge in excessive or binge drinking are more likely to miss work and school. This, in turn, causes an impact on finances and the stability of the family.

Abusive Behavior

Drug addiction can affect your partner's mental health and brain anatomy, affecting how they respond to you in times of conflict. Certain substances, such as alcohol, cocaine, and heroin, create permanent changes in the brain that can cause various mental health problems, including irritability, mood swings, paranoia, anxiety, and depression.

People addicted to drugs are more than twice as likely to suffer from volatile moods and anxiety compared to the general population (Brady et al., 2013). That is not to argue that everyone who uses drugs will eventually become violent and aggressive. A partner addicted to substances has a much higher likelihood of physical, sexual, and psychological assault toward you throughout your relationship.

Codependency

Understanding what role codependency plays in healthy relationships, self-esteem, and self-love is such an important concept that I wrote a book on it. Without getting too far into what I cover in-depth in, ***Stop Being a Doormat and Learn to Love Yourself***, let's get a basic understanding of why codependency is such a dysfunctional behavioral trait and how it leads to toxicity in relationships.

Codependency is a behavioral pattern in which one person has vital physical or emotional needs, and the other spends excessive energy meeting those needs, often at the expense of their well-being.

- Codependency is not a personality disorder. It is a pattern of behavior that incorporates elements of dysfunctional attachment patterns learned in childhood.

- Codependency is a learned behavioral pattern that leads to a person being mentally, emotionally, physically, and spiritually dependent or controlling of another.

- It is an act of depending on or controlling someone to fulfill a psychological requirement for validation.

- It can also overlap with other personality disorders, such as dependent, narcissistic, and borderline personality disorders.

A classic example of a codependent, toxic relationship with a substance abuser is the Caretaker Doormat. The Caretaker Doormat may cover up for an addict, deny there's a problem, and usually fails to provide or maintain boundaries with him. They love him and thrive on being depended on. They enable him by giving him money, shelter, and food, even when they suspect he is using the money to buy more drugs. They cover up problems he causes and may turn a blind eye because admitting a problem exists means they will have to address feelings of guilt and shame. In denial themselves, they try and shield the family and do their best to provide stability and balance in an unpredictable environment. They feel responsible for the addict and what he's dealing with and are soon as dependent on them for reassurance as the addict is on them for enabling behaviors. This enabling role is usually that of a primary caregiver, parent, or partner.

Codependency can easily be repeated in other relationships and can be managed and avoided with mindfulness and awareness of this tendency. Developing self-esteem and self-love and addressing unhealthy behavior patterns can be exceptionally beneficial. I wrote a workbook addressing these elements called, ***Leave that Junk Behind***, wherein you learn practical and insightful methods to change the habitual patterns of negative thinking and low self-esteem reinforcement.

Physical, Mental, or Emotional Abuse

Everyone has disagreements with their spouses, family members, friends, and coworkers. However, there is a clear line between simple conflict and abusive behavior. If your partner's behavior escalates to controlling, physically aggressive, verbally abusive, and emotionally damaging, you are in a hazardous relationship.

Their cruel, abusive behavior has nothing to do with you, and it is not your responsibility to change. Let me repeat that. It has literally <u>nothing to do with you,</u> and it is not your job to try to be extra patient with, provide extra love for, or ever be tolerant of. It is their personality, internal issues, and burden to get a grip on and stop. You can do nothing to "fix this," as so many victims hope for. This should be a hard stop for you and taken very, very seriously.

What is an abusive relationship? An abusive relationship is a pattern of behavior in which one partner uses physical, emotional, verbal, or financial control to harm the other partner. This may include physical violence, sexual assault, threats, intimidation, isolation, and manipulation. It may also include economic abuse, such as controlling access to money or resources. You may have the impression that you have no control over your life or that your partner is exercising complete authority over you.

Research shows that some children raised in abusive families may become aggressive as adults, experience post-traumatic stress disorder, and struggle with depression and other mental health issues throughout their lives (Al Odhayani et al., 2013; Plumptre, 2021; Stiles, 2002). The impact of an abusive relationship doesn't end with you—like venom, its toxicity will spread to your children and other family members, so you should take it very seriously.

Abuse can occur to anyone, at any age, in any form of relationship, no matter the circumstances. Both adults and adolescents are equally at risk of being found in abusive situations. And the fact that you are married to or live with your partner is neither a necessary nor sufficient reason for them to behave aggressively against you.

Physical Abuse

Physical abuse refers to using physical force against another person intending to cause harm or injury. This can include hitting, punching, slapping, choking, pushing, pinching, or using a weapon. This pattern can develop over time, with the abuser starting with minor acts of physical aggression to escalating the severity and frequency of the abuse. The abuser may also likely use other forms of battery, such as emotional and psychological, to further control and manipulate.

- The fact that you are being mistreated or subjected to physical violence is something that victims of physical abuse often strive to keep secret. You may behave differently out of embarrassment, intimidation, or simply because you are unsure how to ask for help.

- You may feel fearful, desperate, scared, ashamed, and depressed by what is happening to you.

- You may heavily medicate with drugs or alcohol to cope with these overwhelming feelings and fears.

- Bruises, broken bones, black eyes, bloody noses, scratches, and abrasions are all basic indicators of physical abuse. You may attempt to hide bruises by covering yourself with clothing or going to different medical professionals for aid.

In a cycle of violence, physical abuse generally escalates over time, with the abuser becoming more violent and the victim becoming more isolated and afraid. The abuser may continuously use physical force to control your movements and limit your access to your family, friends, and other sources of support. This can make it difficult for you to leave the relationship, as you feel trapped and afraid of further harm.

An abusive relationship can also have a profound and lasting impact on the entire family, including children. Children exposed to domestic violence are at an increased risk of a wide range of emotional, behavioral, and physical problems, such as fear, anxiety, and depression. They may also develop behavioral issues, such as aggression, hyperactivity, and difficulty concentrating. Additionally, they may have sleep disturbances, nightmares, and other symptoms associated with post-traumatic stress disorder (Tsavoussis et al., 2014).

Vulnerable children may also experience physical harm if the abuser directly targets them or if they impede the abuser's violence. Children living in an abusive homes may have difficulty forming healthy relationships, have poor self-esteem, and struggle academically. They may also have trouble trusting authority figures and difficulty maintaining healthy relationships in the future. The abuse can hurt the children's relationship with their parents, as they may become distant, detached, or resentful toward the abusive parent.

Psychological Abuse

Psychologically abusive relationships are widespread, misunderstood, and largely undetected. This can be for any number of reasons that we have already discussed as toxic relationship factors. Still, most frequently, it is due to codependency, low self-esteem, and a desire to believe it will "go away" with time and love. Victims often equate abuse as only physical and don't always understand that psychological terror can be even more insidious.

Psychological abuse does not center on a single incident. Instead, it causes a gradual decline in your self-esteem and self-worth, a slow shaving of your confidence, and increased dependency on the abuser. This pervasive pattern of self-esteem annihilation makes it more likely that you will stay with your abuser because you don't feel you are not worthy of anything else.

Years ago, I had to testify in court regarding a child safety case stemming from a severe domestic violence case of psychological and emotional abuse. I was asked to give my opinion if the children in the home should be placed in foster care rather than stay with their mother, who was the victim of the abuse. Their mother, Charlotte, married a manipulative, abusive man named Steven. Steven was a prominent figure in the community and knew he could never physically harm Charlotte and risk leaving visible injury without damaging his reputation. So instead, he chose to sadistically chip away at her self-esteem and insecurity at varying intervals over a period of years, creating invisible, psychological, and emotional wounds that never healed.

He encouraged his young children to disrespect her and told them she was an incompetent mother. He would make fun of her appearance, cooking or intelligence in front of the children and encourage them to laugh at her. When I interviewed her, I found her to be a shell of a woman, unable to think for herself. Steven had brainwashed her to the extent that she believed she had nothing to offer anyone else, was worthless and was lucky to have him take care of her. She felt sorry for him that he had to put up with her and wished her children had a better mother. Part of me wanted to shake and hug her; seeing such a beautiful, vulnerable, broken human was heartbreaking.

During the court hearing, Charlotte would sit in the courtroom and smile at Steven when he would turn to stare at her. She was totally focused on making sure he wasn't angry with her and that she appeared supportive of him as a father. I pointed this out to the judge, who determined that her psychological trauma was so severe that she was temporarily unable to care for her children because she could not care for herself. Her children were removed from the home and sent to live with relatives for some time. With a great deal of therapy, Charlotte began to understand Steve's tremendous psychological control over her and grew to value herself again with support and love from family and friends.

How can you tell if you are being mentally abused? Let's discuss some things to look out for in your relationship.

- **Blame game:** If your partner is an abuser, they will frequently shift the blame for their cruel behavior onto you to strengthen their grip on the relationship.

- **Humiliation:** An abusive partner may make fun of everything, from known insecurities to changes in appearance, to show that they are in charge. They might even do it in public or around their peers to get the most out of the experience and cause the most damage.

- **Name-calling:** A typical strategy employed by abusers to humiliate and degrade their victims is to use abusive language. Your partner may label you foolish, annoying, or embarrassing over minor things. In other situations, they might call you derogatory names for no reason.

- **Making you feel worthless:** Abuse of the mind exploits our fundamental psychological need to maintain a sense of self-worth, such as our pride, happiness, and trust in others. It's demeaning to your self-worth when you are subjected to persistent criticism of your appearance, habitual dismissal of your accomplishments, and disregarding your need for affection.

Emotional Abuse

You may already know visible indications of emotional abuse and manipulation. Still, it's easy to miss these red flags when involved in an emotionally abusive relationship.

Emotional abuse targets you mentally with tactics that create emotional and psychological dependence and confusion. Yelling, loving, and rejecting cyclical behaviors, possessiveness, manipulation, and dismissive of your needs are all forms of emotional abuse. Although no physical contact is involved in this form of abuse, the abuse often begins subtly but quickly escalates and becomes persistent.

Emotional and psychological control tactics can be seen as:

- Demanding to know where you are at all times.

- Yelling and berating you followed by loving words and actions. This is highly manipulative and encourages the victim to associate cruelty with love.

- Jealousy and accusations of cheating without any rational evidence.

- Financially controlling food, clothing, and shelter.

- Disrespectful of personal space and needs.

- Infidelity, disrespecting and devaluing your role as a partner and parent.

- Body shaming and being hypercritical of your appearance.

Abuse in any form is psychologically, emotionally, and physically damaging. It causes long-term damage to your sense of self, your self-esteem, and your mental and physical health. You may not be outwardly injured, but you can suffer from panic attacks, insomnia, eating disorders, and other forms of self-harm to find control in a life controlled by someone else.

Children in an abusive home often suffer silently and they subconsciously learn unhealthy communication and relationship dynamics which later manifest in their own relationships as adults.

Partners leave abusive relationships daily and find housing, financial, and child support in almost every state and country. Starting over feels daunting for many but with support and resources, it becomes much easier to manage and to succeed with. There is help, and it is waiting for you.

Types of Toxic, Doormat Relationships

Now that we know some of the significant characteristics and signs of toxicity in relationships let's look at specific examples of relationships that have developed and display those traits. These may resonate with you, or just parts of them may sound familiar. Either way, it is helpful to understand how the characteristics and symptoms of toxic behavior can evolve into a relationship over time.

Competitive Relationships

Competitive relationships are characterized by a desire to outperform or outdo one another through competition and rivalry. Individuals may strive to prove themselves superior to others. They may also involve a sense of one-upmanship, with each person trying to outdo the other. While competition can be healthy in sports, it can lead to negative feelings, hostility, and insecurity if it focuses on problematic areas of your relationship.

> Kevin and John had been partners for six years. Each was a competitive runner and they enjoyed training together. Eventually, as they each started entering elite races, they started to compete with each other instead of against the other runners. Their sense of mutual support seemed to fade as they became surrounded by an increasing number of elite runners and the competition level increased. Whomever came in behind the other would invariably feel devastated, insecure in their skills and jealous of the other's success.

Some signs of competitive relationships may include:

- Your partner enjoys trying to outperform or outdo you in simple activities or everyday tasks.

    o They may cook a grand meal and exclaim that their cooking is better than yours. If cooking is a source of pride for you, this can be hurtful and lead to feelings of insecurity.

- A constant need by your partner to prove themselves better or worthier than you.

    o This can come in different, subtle forms, but each display chips away your confidence.

- A lack of support or encouragement from your partner for your efforts.

    o When you have a shining moment at work and want to celebrate and be rightfully congratulated, your partner may sulk or complain that his company doesn't treat him well. Suddenly, the evening becomes about them.

- A focus on winning or coming out on top rather than teamwork or collaboration.

    o One parent may feel less important to their children; therefore, they become insecure and will work to "win over" the children to their side with bribery instead of working as a united team.

- A tendency to belittle or diminish your achievements.

    o This is another example of insecurity from one partner bleeding over into their partner's accomplishments. They might say, "Yes, you got a new job, but you only got it because you are a woman, and they needed to fill a quota."

Competitive relationships can feel intense and stressful because you and your partner are vying for the same goal or prize. This can lead both of you to envy and resentment. It's important to remember that healthy competition is a natural and normal part of life and can be a beneficial motivating force. However, if a competitive relationship becomes unhealthy or toxic, it can lead to negative consequences such as damage to your self-esteem, strained friendships, and even physical harm.

One way to manage competitive feelings is to focus on personal growth and self-improvement rather than constantly comparing yourself to others.

Abusive Relationships

As discussed earlier, an abusive relationship is a pattern of behavior in which tactics such as intimidation, manipulation, and control are used to dominate and harm the other person.

Some additional characteristics of abusive relationships may include:

- **Sexual abuse:** Your partner may use sexual coercion, manipulation, or assault to control you.

- **Humiliation:** Your partner may belittle you, shame you, mock you in front of others, or make you feel guilty or worthless.

- **Control:** Your partner may try to control your actions, decisions, or behaviors, such as whom you can see or talk to, what you can wear, or where you can go.

- **Threats:** Your partner may threaten you directly or indirectly or use intimidation to control you.

- **Isolation:** Your access to the outside world can become restricted, and your partner will try to deny you the opportunity to see your family or friends.

Being in an abusive relationship can be a grueling experience. It can involve feeling trapped, isolated, afraid, and unsafe. It can lead to a sense of powerlessness and fear of what might happen to you if you try to leave or stand up for yourself.

It's also possible to feel guilty or ashamed for not being able to leave or for not being able to make your partner see how you are suffering. You may feel you are to blame for the abuse or that you are not worthy of love or respect. You may also feel you have no one to turn to for help or that no one will believe you if you seek help.

It's important to remember that being in an abusive relationship is not your fault. If you are in one or experiencing any of the behaviors discussed thus far, please consider reaching out to a trusted friend, family member, or professional for support and guidance.

Narcissistic Based Relationships

In recent years, narcissism and its destructive personality traits have gained greater recognition as a popular source of severe problems in a relationship. I frequently hear individuals refer to a partner, family member, or co-worker as "narcissistic" when describing a selfish person.

In short, narcissistic individuals are profoundly insecure. They live in a world of "Me, myself, and I." They require excessive validation and admiration, feel superior to others, and cannot meet anyone else's needs unless it benefits them somehow. Have you ever met someone who walks into a room and somehow manages to get all the attention focused on themselves? Do you feel emotionally depleted when you are around them, feel ignored, or are in a loop of pleasing them and disregarding your feelings? In my book, **Stop Being a Doormat and Learn to Love Yourself,** I review how narcissistic traits are significant indicators of codependent dynamics in relationships and how to recognize and manage them. They generally go hand-in-hand with one another.

Narcissists are master manipulators at getting others to do their bidding and care for them first and foremost. The gaslighting can be very subtle, but through expert emotional manipulation, you will find yourself in an exceptionally dysfunctional and toxic relationship.

Narcissists also have difficulty maintaining healthy and meaningful relationships, as they cannot see the needs and feelings of others as equally important to their own. They may have a history of short-lived relationships, multiple marriages, unstable employment history, and few if any, long-term friends. When questioned, they will quickly blame others for their problems and failed relationships and never assume responsibility. If someone has a narcissistic personality, there isn't a cure, but therapy can help bring about behavioral awareness and work to recognize others' needs.

The following are warning signs that you may be involved with a narcissist:

- Your partner is overly self-involved and lacks genuine empathy toward others.

- They are generally not interested in your feelings or needs and are more concerned with their own needs and desires, even above their children's.

- They may belittle or criticize you and not accept criticism themselves.

- They are prone to fits of irrational anger or rage and cannot regulate their emotions.

- They have an exaggerated sense of self-importance. They may constantly boast about their accomplishments and feel entitled to the best of everything.

- You find you are constantly trying to meet your partner's needs and that your own needs and feelings are ignored. You may also feel like you are being used or taken advantage of and cannot have a genuine and meaningful connection with your partner.

I was once in a short, *very short,* dating relationship with a man who was a true narcissist. He displayed so many red flags on our first date that I lost count. In fact, he asked what the word narcissistic implied and why people always called him that. He was charming and attentive, but it was very superficial. He never really asked me about myself. I told him I had a bad day at work and was frustrated, and he just talked about his day, never acknowledging what I said or my obvious need to vent.

I also observed that he had no real long or short-term friends. When I asked whom he spent time with, he would say, "Oh, I tried befriending some neighbors, but they were jerks." He also bad-mouthed his family as being uninvolved in his life and selfish.

He had been an actor 20 years prior, acting in minor roles in a handful of B-list movies and tv shows. It never amounted to any fame or success, but, entertainingly so, he would inflate his career to the point of absurdity. When talking to anyone new, these straight-to-video movies become blockbuster hits. He managed to interject stories of his "great success" into conversations. I would mention the hot weather, and he would say, "Back during the filming of my action movie, it was hot like this all the time, and I had to work hard to stay in character." When we ate dinner with his children, I watched them roll their eyes and look at each other every time the conversation about their lives turned into another story about his acting days. They were familiar with his behavior.

After four dates, I realized I was so impressed by the depth of his narcissism that I saw him more as a case study than as viable partner potential. I ended our contact, much to his shock and dismay.

It's important to remember that no relationship is perfect and that everyone has flaws. However, if you feel like your partner's behavior is causing you distress or making it difficult for you to be your true self, feel overwhelmed, or be supported, it may be worth reevaluating your choices!

Antisocial Based Relationships

Antisocial personality disorder, often referred to as psychopathy or sociopathy, is characterized by a lack of empathy, impulsive behavior, and a tendency to manipulate and exploit others for personal gain. While recognizable and often used, psychopathy and sociopathy are not medical terms recognized in the Diagnostic and Statistical Manual of Mental Disorders (DSM-5). Instead, the DSM-5 uses the term *antisocial personality disorder* to describe individuals who exhibit a pattern of disregard or violation of the rights of others.

These individuals are skilled at charm and manipulation and may use these tactics to engage with you. It's not uncommon for individuals with antisocial tendencies to form relationships, although they may be characterized by exploitation. These individuals can be highly educated, outwardly successful, and seemingly confident people. However, these relationships can be harmful and one-sided, as partners with antisocial tendencies are incapable of genuine feelings of love or care for another person. They will use people for their benefit and are often prone to infidelity, abuse, and other forms of scheming and persuasion. Individuals with antisocial personality traits will invariably have narcissistic traits and vice versa. The handsome, charming serial killer Ted Bundy was a perfect example of an anti-social narcissist.

Here are potential warning signs that you may be in a toxic, doormat relationship with an antisocial individual:

- **Lack of empathy**: Your partner may seem indifferent to your feelings and may not understand or care about how you feel.

- **Manipulative or controlling behavior**: Your partner may try to persuade, gaslight, and control you, making you feel responsible for their actions.

- **Impulsivity**: Your partner may act on their impulses without considering the consequences and engage in risky or dangerous behavior.

- **Lack of remorse or guilt**: Your partner does not feel guilty about hurting you or others and does not show remorse for their actions.

- **Callousness**: Your partner may seem unemotional or uncaring and doesn't show concern for your welfare, family, or friends.

A relationship with a narcissist or antisocial individual can be emotionally and mentally draining on you and potentially dangerous. You may constantly feel on edge and unaware of your partner's true motivations or intentions. You must honestly examine your history and reasons for being in a relationship with this type of person. Recognizing these traits and warning signs will enable you to move on to healthier and safer relationships.

Now that we have identified what toxic relationships can look like, we will discuss recovering and moving beyond these unhealthy experiences in the next chapter.

Chapter 3:

Recovering from Doormat

Relationships and Marriages

"People who wonder if the glass is half empty or full miss the point. The glass is refillable - Unknown."

There is usually more than one reason marriages don't last, and you are not alone. Statistics show that nearly 20% of marriages fail within the first five years (Mason, 2022). When a marriage or long-term relationship ends, feelings of denial, anger, sadness and a sense of failure are all normal emotions you may experience during this grief process.

Marriage is simply a union of two imperfect people who live together with their imperfections. Identifying the root causes of your relationship's breakdown is the first step to not repeating them. Answering these questions and identifying any toxic warning signs we have already reviewed can help you move forward confidently and establish the life you want.

We are not born with relationship-ending coping skills. These are learned through life experiences and circumstances. It is unreasonable to think you can handle this alone without a few stumbles.

Where Do We Go Now?

Divorce, like any other breakup, can be challenging to cope with. It brings anger, low self-esteem, hurt feelings, and rejection. It can take months to years to recover from the effects of divorce. Though the journey to recovery may be challenging, there is always light and happiness at the end of the tunnel, especially if you embrace the change and possibilities of a new life.

When I divorced, I grieved the loss of a life I envisioned, felt guilt for my children, and had many sad, doubting days. But deep down, I was relieved that I could set my life back on a positive course and provide a healthy example for my children. I remember standing in line at a grocery store and wanting to burst into tears. Nothing had happened; I just felt a sudden, overwhelming sadness. I sat in my car, took a deep breath, and realized it was just part of the change process and that it was perfectly okay to be angry, sad, or even happy. You can get through this. It takes the support of others, motivation to make positive changes and a deep belief that it can only get better.

How to Ride the Rollercoaster of Divorce and Breakups

If your relationship's glue doesn't hold up the walls of your relationship, you should at least stand firm after the walls collapse. It's not easy to stand firm because you may have memories that take you back to a point when you and your loved one were in a good place and felt they were all you needed. Fear of the unknown, worrying about going back to work, finding a new, and being a single parent are other factors that make divorce one of the most stressful events in a person's life.

Here are some activities and tips that can be useful during the recovery process:

Accept It

When you get married, the thoughts of divorce don't come into play. It sometimes comes as a shock and leaves you in disbelief when it happens. It's hard to accept and understand that your partner no longer loves you. Acceptance that your marriage is not working is the most crucial awareness step in recovery. Although it might be uncomfortable, this step is your "light bulb" moment, as it will allow you to start the transition in your mind and grow to accept it as necessary.

Talk About It

A problem shared is a problem half solved. Talking about your divorce with family, friends, online support groups, and trained professionals will help you recover. Knowing you are not alone in this process is a potent healing tool. Keep close to those who help you in difficult times and those who support you unconditionally.

Co-Parenting Success

As you and your partner prepare to separate and have children together, it is essential to consider your children's pending experience. Divorce affects everyone, and it is possible to create a positive example for your children to learn from. To avoid problems, anxiety, and confusion, you and your partner must learn how to be effective co-parents, as this is a lifetime situation. Conflict-free co-parenting plays a significant role in cushioning the stress of divorce on children and you.

Seek Professional Help

It is easy to lose yourself to depression, resentment, low self-esteem, and anxiety during this significant life change. Talking to professionals and like-minded individuals about your feelings and emotions helps relieve stress and open up an opportunity for them to help you through the process. Licensed professional therapists and online groups will give you practical advice on coping with your new life and valuable tips about the logistics of your divorce.

Wait for Yourself to Heal

A divorce will bring you a lot of mixed feelings about life and relationships in particular. Heartbreak has a funny way of playing with people's emotions and mindsets. Avoid rushing into a new relationship before you get your mind clear as to what you want and don't want moving forward. Don't let the fear of never finding love again cloud your mind or set you off on the journey toward healing. Remember, divorce doesn't have to be the end of your love life; you can view it as a new opportunity to find someone with whom you will be genuinely compatible.

Reconnect With Passions

Reconnecting with your interests and discovering new ones is essential in recovery. Remind yourself of the old passions that put a smile on your face and brought you happiness. These passions may include dancing, painting, or joining a sports team. Focus on staying busy and keeping your mind occupied rather than being alone.

Michael, a father of two, shared how swimming and meditating helped him during his divorce recovery process. After parting ways with his partner of six years, he was devastated. He felt so broken that he couldn't even recognize himself anymore. His therapist helped him rekindle his interest in the activities he used to love. It gave him a new daily goal, brought him pleasure and stress relief, and aided his personal development as a single man.

Take Care of Yourself

As you go through this recovery phase, spoil yourself with the nice things life offers. Get yourself a gift, eat healthy food, and stimulate your physical activity. Try to avoid making significant and radical life decisions and stick to a healthy routine as much as possible. However, don't lose yourself in the quest for fun and personal happiness. Be wary of harmful and toxic behaviors such as consuming too much alcohol, among other impulsive, self-medicating strategies.

Avoid Negative Patterns With Your Ex-Spouse

The recovery process requires that you rid your life of bad habits and replace them with good ones. It follows the saying, "Out with the old, in with the new." As you move on with your life, you and your spouse are bound to meet or interact, especially if you have children or live in the same town. As you meet, pay attention to your interactions and discussions to avoid unnecessary tension and falling back into old patterns. Keeping the dialogue to pertinent topics keeps you focused.

Let Yourself Off the Hook

Don't be too hard on yourself after a divorce. Remember, you are not the first person to end a marriage or relationship, and you won't be the last. You might not be functioning at your best, and you may be less productive at work. No one is immune to this feeling; everyone experiences it to a degree. Time, self-love, and patience are essential in healing.

The journey to recovery from divorce is complex and lengthy. You will face challenges as you recover, but it is essential to remember that you are moving forward from what was dysfunctional and unhappy to an entirely new future that will be what you want it to be. There may be moments during the recovery process when you consider returning to your partner. Change can be scary and challenging, and even though it is toxic, the old relationship is familiar. During this phase, you should carefully weigh the temptation to get back together for convenience against the reasons you divorced. Don't lose sight of what drove the desire for change. Invest your energy in self-love and self-care, which we will cover in the next chapter.

Chapter 4:

Building Confidence and

Optimism

"Once we believe in ourselves, we can risk curiosity, wonder, spontaneous delight, or any experience that reveals the human spirit"—e e cummings.

Finding Your Confidence and Self-Esteem Again

Trusting yourself and your capabilities is what confidence is all about. It is essential to your health and psychological well-being. When you develop confidence, you gain control over your life. You face your problems boldly, with a positive outlook, and are not deterred by people who don't bring you fulfillment.

After going through an unhealthy relationship, your self-esteem may feel shattered beyond repair. When you are in a relationship with a toxic person, they systematically tear down your feelings of self-confidence and self-worth to the point that it's damaging to your mental sanity. It takes time to repair this. Be kind to yourself. We, especially women, are our own worst critics. We often see ugliness, incompetence, and weakness, whereas others see beauty, strength, and competence.

Self-esteem is how you see yourself and think and feel about who you are. It is closely tied in with your self-respect and confidence. You likely have healthy self-esteem if you see life with a positive outlook and look forward to each day and new experiences. If you dread new challenges, find it difficult to get up and go, struggle to find pleasure in the small things, and constantly criticize yourself, then the opposite is true.

When people cause damage to your sense of self, a cycle of negative thought patterns can begin. You start feeling bad about yourself. Thoughts of wishing you were more confident, capable, or had more backbone make you start perceiving yourself as weak. This creates a sense of self-loathing, causing you to lose self-respect, and your self-esteem plummets even lower. You feel hopeless; it feels as if people have taken advantage of you for so long that you don't know how to change it, and you let it continue.

Somewhere, your self-esteem took a severe knock, but like a crumbled building, you can rebuild it into what you envision for your future self. Think of your self-esteem as a project, and you are the project manager. The foundations you were born with are still there, so it is entirely doable.

If you are in an unhealthy relationship—romantic, familial, or platonic—someone will try and pull you down with them. Misery loves company, after all.

Re-building your self-esteem can seem huge, so start small with baby steps. It took you a long time to get here, so be patient with yourself.

Steps To Rebuilding Confidence and Self-Esteem

As you start your life anew, there are certain things that confident people do regularly that you can incorporate into your daily life and attitude to build up your self-esteem and confidence levels.

- Believe in yourself.

  This seems simple, but it is difficult for many people who struggle with insecurity and low self-esteem. Look at areas in your life where you have been successful, whether securing a specific job, finishing college, raising happy children, or anything else you can say you and you alone accomplished. It is a slippery slope to losing confidence in yourself if you don't believe you have accomplished anything.

- Know your strengths and talents. Set new goals for yourself.

  Confidence is often developed with positive achievements. Achieving small and large goals will create the space for you to feel good about yourself. Create a new plan to accomplish today, this week, this month, and this year. They can be as simple as reading a book or losing 5 lbs.—anything to give you a sense of accomplishment and a well-done job. We can't always rely on others for a pat on the back, so be your own champion.

- Monitor your goal progress.

  Make a running list and check each goal or aspiration as completed. It is also essential to come up with quantifiable goals. Meaning, break down important goals into small ones. So instead of saying, "Get a promotion or lose 50 pounds", keep a running spreadsheet of what you eat, the number of minutes you exercise each day, and the projects completed at work. List the projects and tasks you have completed that will work toward each goal. Watching your upward trajectory toward success visually is motivating and an excellent opportunity to find positive reinforcement.

- Help others and do the right thing.

  Most confident people follow a value and moral system and make decisions and choices based on these values. Your actions and decisions define who you are.

- Make a list of your strengths and talents.

  You love to garden and can grow incredible roses. You are a thoughtful and kind friend to those in need. You are a firefighter and in great shape and can easily carry injured people and save lives. You are a great public speaker and love volunteering to read to seniors.

- Stand up for yourself!

  In the past, you might have taken the passive, codependent route and let others decide for you even if you secretly disagreed. No more! Speak up and take a stand for what you want, what is best for you, and what you believe in. Remember that you are worthy and deserve what you want in life.

- Stop overthinking!

  Confident people are decisive and stick to their instincts. Unless it is a life-or-death decision, it can be fixed. Go with your gut and build on this new, determined self.

- Find a new hobby you enjoy; you may be good at it if you try.

  I once went to an archery range with a friend. I had never tried it before and thought it would be a new and fun thing to learn. I remember standing there, all geared up, holding this giant compound bow, laughing, and saying to my friend, "I am going to be so bad at this!"

  That was an unfounded, automatic negative thought based on insecurity in my untested abilities. What would have been better to say is, "I may be horrible at first, but it's my first time, and I am going to have fun trying." I ended up being reasonably good at it. Who knew? I walked away from the range feeling happy and confident that I had tried something different and found a new talent.

- Follow through and be fearless.

  If you say you will do something, then do it and believe in yourself. Is there a trip you've always wanted to take by yourself? Read up about it, make plans, and then do it. Is there something you were frightened of doing but secretly wished you could? Look your fear in the face and do it. As long as it is not mortally dangerous and you are not hurting yourself or others, there's no reason why you can't at least give it a try. Step outside your comfort zone and thrive.

- Perseverance to the end.

  Perseverance is critical to building self-confidence. It is about knowing your self-worth and staying on track toward your goals. For example, I have never been a fan of long-distance running. Some irritating people are natural runners who can churn out five or ten miles at a time without pain or misery, and they happily achieve that elusive runner's high. Sadly, I am not one of those people. I only run to stay in shape and have never experienced euphoria unless you count the happiness when the run has ended. All these negative thoughts creep into my head during a run, allowing me the excuse to walk, tie my shoes for the 5th time, or not push myself to keep improving. As an athlete, I understand the training practices to employ to be successful, but my body and mind are only somewhat open to them.

  A few years ago, I wanted to compete in a triathlon with a group of friends and knew I needed to change my mindset about running to accomplish this feat. I joined a running group to hold myself accountable and created personal goals to achieve during each run (making it .25, .5, 1, 2, 4, and eventually 5 miles without stopping). I eventually competed in over eight triathlons due to this mind shift. I learned to stick with it in the face of resistance from outside and internal forces, and I can now regularly apply this practice of perseverance to other areas of my life.

- Know your value.

  If you've carved a good piece of woodwork, don't undercharge because people are hesitant. Someone somewhere wants what you are selling, and you want to walk away with a profit.

- Don't be afraid to ask for help.

  Confident people don't take on commitments they know they can't accomplish, and if a challenge arises, they ask for assistance.

- Set realistic goals.

  Do you know the adage about eating an elephant one bite at a time? As codependent people often over-extend themselves, practice committing to only what you are sure you can deliver.

- Set personal goals and stick with them.

  If you want to learn a new language but don't have much time, find an app that allows you to learn in short segments. Set aside five minutes a day, possibly at the same time, and you will reach your goal without realizing it.

  One significant advantage of setting realistic targets is that each goal you achieve boosts your confidence, giving you the drive to aim even higher!

  The same applies to finding the confidence to move on from a bad relationship. Outline your targets for the future, assess them for feasibility, then work hard till you achieve the goals.

Confident vs. Doormat

Knowing the difference between a confident person and a doormat (non-confident person) can help you see where you stand and how you can make changes. Here are some easy differences to think about:

Confident people are often:

- open-minded

- optimistic

- decisive

- willing to admit mistakes

- fun to be around

- ready to celebrate other people's progress

- free to learn and grow

- happy with themselves and don't change to make others happy

Doormats are often:

- pessimistic

- indecisive

- closed-minded

- quick to hide flaws

- love to make excuses

- jealous of others

- insecure

- have poor body images

- will twist themselves out of shape to make others happy

Eliminating Negative Thoughts

Coming from an unhealthy relationship that has battered your self-esteem and allowed negative thought patterns to take over is another battle to address. Automatic, negative thought patterns originate after repeated narratives play on a loop in your mind. Sometimes you create these habitual thoughts based on lifelong insecurities, and sometimes, they are learned due to dysfunctional experiences.

- I am not smart enough.

- I wish I weren't so fat.

- I am not a good parent.

- I wish I were better at my job.

It is critical to start identifying these habitual patterns of negative thoughts so that you can learn to interrupt them before they take hold. Once you start noticing just one negative thought pattern, you'll pick up on it every time you think or say it and begin to break this nasty habit.

Set aside time when you won't be disturbed, get a journal or notepad (I use both so I can paste notes to myself on the refrigerator or my mirror), and write down your feelings about some automatic negative thoughts you have had recently. Can you identify when it first started? Was it something that happened, or did somebody say something? Picture the situation and see if you can remember what occurred.

Here are automatic, negative thought patterns I often hear from others:

- Body shaming yourself every time you look in the mirror.

- When telling others your relationship ended, you blame yourself.

- Thinking you are stupid because you struggle to learn the new computer program at work. Everyone else has mastered it, so you must be too incompetent to understand.

- Waking up and dreading the workday before it has even started.

- Jumping to conclusions about why your boyfriend hasn't called or texted in a day, immediately assuming it has something to do with you.

- Feeling nervous about speaking up in a meeting because you might be wrong or embarrassed.

- Deciding there is no way you will be considered for this promotion. There are so many other people more qualified than you. Why even bother?

Use this exercise to practice changing the negative thoughts you wrote down. You are training your brain to pause after the nasty critic pops in and consider an alternative pattern.

Let's look at the above examples; here are alternatively positive and productive ideas to counter the negative ones:

- I don't feel great about my weight, but I am excited to see my body change over the next five months as I exercise and change my eating habits. I love those before and after pictures, and I will do some too. Everyone has a different shape, and I am going to embrace mine. It doesn't happen in a day, and it will feel good to see the results down the road.

- Unfortunately, my relationship ended, but there were severe problems, and I am happier now.

- I don't quite understand this new software program, but to be fair, I haven't tried to learn it, and I've been busy with other tasks. It can't be impossible to learn. I need to focus and maybe get a quick personal review from the tech team. I am not stupid and will learn it just like everyone else.

- You wake up and think, "Great! It's a new day. I have to go to work, so I am determined to find something good about it and won't let it get me down."

- My boyfriend hasn't called yet, but who cares. I know he loves me. He is probably busy and said he would call when he could. I should get active, too, so I stop dwelling on this and making myself unnecessarily crazy.

- I have good ideas, and I bring value to this company. I refuse to be intimidated when my colleagues are friendly and open-minded and would never laugh at me if I am wrong. If they do, then I will laugh too.

- I am going to go for this promotion. I don't care if I am not the most qualified. It will give me practice interviewing and show my bosses that I am eager for a management track. If I don't get it, then it's not a loss. I'll ask for feedback as to what I need to do to get it next time.

Gradually, you will automatically identify your negative thoughts, speech, or patterns through repetition and practice. Think of each negative belief as an opportunity. You've already got your mind programmed to spot them. When you put a particular car on your wish list, you start seeing them everywhere—the same model in the same color. Your brain picks up on what we tell it, consciously and subconsciously. Your self-esteem is growing, and like a seedling, nurture it until it thrives.

Employers often ask job applicants to list their weaknesses and strengths. Isn't it always easier to list negative things about ourselves;

many of us are at a loss and uncomfortable having to write down the positive attributes.

Grab that journal again. You already know all your habitual negative attributes, so write down one positive thing about yourself. It could be as simple as having beautiful eyes, good dress sense, and a great singing voice. Or you may be a talented cook, designer, or gardener. Perhaps you are great at your job or were top of your class in school.

If you can't think of anything, then think of your family, friends, and even strangers who have complimented you and remember how wonderful it felt. Write down what they said, even if you must go back to your childhood and grade school teacher. Add a new positive attribute daily, or pick every second day or twice a week—do whatever is going to work for you and do it consistently.

I have found that identifying, understanding, and stopping negative thought patterns is crucial to building a stronger sense of self and promoting self-love. Behavioral and thought change doesn't happen overnight; we all need help unlearning these unwanted habits. As a result, I created the workbook **Leave That Junk Behind** to address these self-esteem issues with practical and fun exercises.

The next chapter will review how to continue your growth, set boundaries, and let go of the negative people in your life.

Chapter 5:

Starting Over and Establishing

New Boundaries

*"Don't waste your energy trying to change opinions ... Do your thing, and don't care
if they like it."—Tina Fey*

Relationships can sometimes reach a point where letting go is better
than holding on. Although it is hard to let go of someone you have
invested so much time in, it can also be an opportunity to start a new
life and establish new boundaries.

When evaluating past mistakes or unhealthy patterns you want to avoid
in the future, consider what has happened and how your thoughts or
behaviors played a role. Do you have a pattern of dating emotionally
unavailable individuals? Do you have codependency traits? Does your
self-esteem or confidence play a role in determining the type of person
you typically date? You can't control how your date or partner behaves
and are never responsible for their behavior, but you can control how
you respond.

Trust Your Gut

There are no guarantees with relationships, but by taking the time to
listen to yourself and considering your options before making a final
decision, you will be more able to trust that it's the right path for you.
Trust your gut, do not ignore what it's telling you. You may be attuned
to more red flags or warning signs than you know.

Remember the story I told you about dating the narcissist, ex-actor? I
had red flags about him within an hour of meeting him. I gave him a

chance because I was willing to give him the benefit of the doubt. Maybe he was just nervous. But I am not so nice or lacking in self-worth that I would let myself enter into a relationship with someone so selfish and self-absorbed. I listened to my gut and avoided wasting time and energy.

Trusting your gut can also help you feel more confident about starting a new life and setting healthy boundaries. When you rely on your instincts and follow your heart, you may be more likely to feel at peace with your decision, even if it is difficult.

Forgive Yourself

When considering life-changing decisions, it is essential to take the time to forgive yourself for any mistakes or wrongdoings that you may have committed in the past. We are human, and we make mistakes. The key is learning from them to move forward and heal.

Let me tell you the story of Alice, a successful businesswoman in her mid-40s.

> Alice is ambitious and has a career that she loves. She has also been married and divorced twice. After her second divorce, Alice tried to move on with her romantic life, but she couldn't forgive herself. She blamed herself for the divorces and carried guilt and shame for their failure. She was also fearful of repeating mistakes and entering into another unhealthy relationship.

> Alice eventually went to a therapist because she was dissatisfied with her life and her fears of moving forward. Through therapy, she learned that she tended to date men who were emotionally distant and controlling, and their mutual codependency would always lead to unhappiness. She knew that it was not entirely her fault, that sometimes relationships don't work out, and being aware of her patterns and habits was the first step in setting her on a healthier path.

Ending a destructive relationship and finding a new trajectory for your life again is something to look forward to. You are taking charge, and the future is what you make it!

Don't be overly critical when you feel tempted to fall back into the patterns you are trying to change. Step back, look at why you felt that way or dropped into an old habit, and adjust. It is okay to fail today; you can always try again tomorrow. You will get it right if you believe you can, and trust me; you can.

This is your life, and it is full of adventure. Think of it like a movie. The main character either has a clear plan or none at all. They're thrown a curveball, a challenge, or some drama and must change and adapt as the movie plot unfolds. We are the actors in our movies. You decide the genre. Is it drama, action, adventure, or inspirational?

Setting New and Realistic Boundaries

Setting boundaries can also help reduce stress by limiting the time and energy spent on people or activities that drain you. Clear boundaries can improve communication by allowing you to express your needs and limitations openly to others. Healthy self-esteem and confidence can make setting boundaries easier, professionally and personally.

Work Boundaries

Self-esteem and confidence can make it easier to set new boundaries at work because they can give you the belief of your worth and value as an individual. When you have a positive sense of self-worth, you are more likely to feel comfortable standing up for yourself and advocating for your needs and boundaries. This can be especially important in a professional setting where it's easy to feel pressured to take on more responsibilities or to put the needs of others before your own.

Mark started a new job at an investment firm. He was eager to prove himself and become indispensable to his management and was more than willing to pitch in anywhere he could. After one year on the job, Mark found that he was routinely expected to arrive early, leave late, and take over work from others struggling to meet quotas. Wanting to be perceived as cooperative and willing, he never complained or questioned this expectation. After another year of being asked to work 70 hours a week, he decided to speak to his boss. His boss was genuinely surprised Mark was unhappy and told him he should have said something earlier. He told Mark that he gave off the impression that he wanted and liked the extra work and promised to reduce it. Mark was sorry he didn't speak up sooner and realized that no one else would if he didn't value his worth and time.

Personal Boundaries

Have you ever had a time when a date or friend was routinely late for a get-together, and you never really complained? Ever experienced a relationship where your partner didn't respect your private time and insisted you accommodate their needs? Do you ever feel like you give and give to others, and they don't return the same effort? If you answered yes to any of these, or thought of a similar situation, then setting personal boundaries should be a goal for you.

David wants to repair his car and needs help, but his partner, Brian, doesn't have the time to help. David manipulates Brian by appearing sad and upset, thereby making Brian feel responsible for his disappointment. Despite being too busy and overwhelmed at work, Brian feels obligated to help, avoid a fight, and keep David happy.

Self-esteem and strong self-confidence are critical to achieving and setting personal boundaries. When someone doesn't know they are offending you, taking advantage of you, or being insensitive, only you can tell them you don't like that.

Confidence can give you the courage to assert your boundaries, even in difficult or uncomfortable situations. When you are confident in yourself and your abilities, you are more likely to feel secure in your decisions and to stand up for yourself and your needs.

Family Boundaries

Self-esteem and confidence are also essential factors in setting family boundaries. When you have healthy self-esteem and confidence, you are more likely to feel comfortable asserting your needs and limits and less likely to let family members take advantage of you. Sometimes, because they are family, individuals will overstep common courtesy because of their relationship with you. There is a subtle, unspoken assumption that you sacrifice willingly for your family. They may ask for money, food, and shelter and never pay you back or leave your couch. Depending on how this impacts you and your life, consider speaking up for yourself and limiting what you are willing to provide.

> Erin came from a close family of five, all living within one mile of each other. Erin, a natural caregiver, was always willing to lend a hand to her elderly parents. Erin's siblings also enjoyed that Erin liked to care for others and were thrilled they didn't have to give up their weekends running errands for their parents. They were also happy to let Erin cook at every major holiday and host family gatherings at her house. Erin never complained because it initially felt great to be needed and appreciated. Lately, though, Erin started to feel resentful of her siblings. She was frustrated that they placed so much responsibility on her and never offered to help. By reviewing her habits of never speaking up, never requiring her siblings to share responsibilities, and never standing up for herself, Erin realized that she had also allowed her siblings to take advantage of her kind nature.

When Setting Boundaries Is Difficult

When you are insecure, codependent, or low in self-confidence, you probably find it difficult to set boundaries in any area of your life. There is a fear that setting firm boundaries could cause someone to leave or become angry with you. They might never ask for your help again, and you would lose that warm, codependent feeling of being needed and wanted. You may fear confrontation because you worry about the consequences of speaking up or expressing your views and damaging relationships.

Financial Issues in a Toxic Relationship

It's challenging to set boundaries when financially dependent on someone, especially if you are considering getting a divorce or are receiving support via your divorce agreement. You may worry that everything will crumble if you upset them.

> Kate had been married to her husband, Mike, for 15 years. They had three children together and relied on Mike's income to support their family. However, their marriage had been rocky for a while, and they were both unhappy and unfulfilled. She wanted to leave the marriage but was afraid to do so because her financial situation depended on Mike, and she had no idea how to support herself and her children to the same level.
>
> One day, Kate met with a therapist specializing in relationships and boundaries. The therapist helped her understand the importance of setting boundaries and advocating for herself, even in an emotionally charged situation. With the therapist's support, Kate spoke with Mike about her feelings. She told him she was unhappy in the marriage and wanted to make a change.
>
> Unfortunately, Mike was not receptive to Kate's feelings and refused to work on the issues in their marriage. Kate realized she needed to prioritize her and her children's well-being, and

she left the marriage despite being financially unstable. It was a hard decision, but Kate knew it was the right one for her.

Kate found a job and worked hard to provide for her children. She found her new life fulfilling and meaningful. While it was a challenging transition, Kate was grateful that she set boundaries and advocated for herself, which allowed her to pursue her own happiness and create a better future for herself and her children.

Looking at Kate's story, it's helpful to have an open and honest conversation about your needs and boundaries with the person you might be financially dependent on. Be clear about what you are comfortable with and what you need to feel supported. Don't be afraid to seek the support of an attorney, friend, therapist, or other trusted professional as you navigate this challenging time.

Consider what you want your future to look like and start making plans to make it a reality—set goals for budgeting, saving, and paying off debts. Invest time and effort in learning how to handle your finances to improve your assertiveness in setting money-related boundaries. Consider discussing your situation with a financial planner or seeking additional education or training to help you build a stronger financial foundation. Speaking to a professional like a financial advisor can provide an objective perspective, help you work through any fears or concerns, plan for the future, and become more financially independent, even if that means making tough decisions in the short term.

Dumping the Doormat and Setting Boundaries With Your Ex

Above all, you need to set clear boundaries with the person you are ending things with. This means discussing how and if you will continue to communicate. If children are involved, this needs to be established right away. Some parents can openly call and text each other without issues. Others need to do the child custody exchange at a police department due to volatility concerns. Other instances may arise as you and your ex start new relationships. For example, if your ex-partner remarries, are you okay with them visiting the kids with their new partner?

It's helpful to set goals for yourself before and during difficult times in a relationship. Please don't be too hard on yourself; taking things one step at a time is okay. Be sure to reach out for help when needed, and do not let other people hold you back as you set goals for your future. When planning to move on, shift your focus toward what's to come. With the right attitude, setting new goals can be an empowering experience that enables you to create growth opportunities. Remember that the goals you set should focus on self-care, align with your values, and provide flexible options for personal growth.

As part of the goal-setting process, it is also essential to reflect on past mistakes, identify areas that need improvement, and acknowledge any successes along the way. Doing so will help you gain clarity about what you want in life and how you plan to achieve those goals in the future without constantly looking back.

Chapter 6

You've Ditched the Doormat

"How you love yourself is how you teach others to love you."- Rupi Kaur

Putting Yourself First Is Not Selfish

Retraining your brain is the path to healing yourself so you can flourish and your world with you.

Putting yourself first means recognizing that you have requirements that must be taken care of. There is no reason why you shouldn't make your needs a priority. You've heard flight attendants on planes tell you to put your mask on before your children in case of an emergency. It makes sense that by ensuring your needs are met (have oxygen first), you can assist others. If incapacitated, exhausted, or depressed, you are not in an ideal position or fully capable of helping anyone else.

You are always your number one priority. Seeking your happiness means you will have more energy, bring positivity to the table, and likely be more productive at work.

If you are healthy and happy, you can better cope with life's challenges and be there for your loved ones. It is a win-win for everyone.

Develop Healthy Relationships

Healthy relationships can be beneficial after a hard time with your partner. Whether it be friendships, family, work, or romance, getting grounded and reaffirming that great relationships are out, there is very rewarding. It provides hope that it can be better.

Your relationships need boundaries to be healthy without disrespecting the people you interact with. Establishing and respecting boundaries is important because this helps prevent conflicts and ensures both parties feel heard and valued.

Overall, take time for yourself, prioritize self-care, and give yourself time to relax and recharge. By developing healthy ways to interact with the people around you, you can work toward strengthening your relationships as you move on from a toxic one. Always remind yourself that it's never too late to change the role you play in relationships.

Creating Realistic Perspectives and Priorities

Creating realistic perspectives and priorities can help you focus on what is most important to you and work toward achieving your goals in a meaningful and fulfilling way. You can start by focusing on your needs and thinking about what is most important and what you need to feel happy and fulfilled.

- **Consider the long term.** Take care of your physical and emotional well-being, as this can help you feel more grounded and better able to handle the challenges ahead. Plan what you want to achieve in the short and long term; that will give you a good road map.

- **Be open to compromise.** Unpredictable changes after a divorce or breakup are inevitable. Divorce involves compromises and finding solutions that work for both parties.

Setting new priorities can help you stay motivated and focused and prevent you from feeling overwhelmed or frustrated. It can also allow you to explore new possibilities that may have been previously unavailable. By setting priorities and a realistic perspective, you will focus on rebuilding your life and finding greater happiness.

Executing Plans for a Happier You

Making positive health and social wellness changes and practicing self-care are challenging after an unhealthy relationship. By executing plans for a more robust, healthier life, you reinforce that your health and happiness are priorities in your new life. It shows that you deserve to be treated with respect and kindness and that you won't tolerate situations that suffocate your well-being.

Practice Self-Care

Taking care of your physical and emotional well-being is always important in life. Some self-care practices you may want to consider include:

- exercising

- eating a healthy diet every day

- getting enough sleep

- taking breaks

- practicing mindfulness

- finding new hobbies, you enjoy

- meditate

- use art therapy to relax and unwind

- adopt a pet and discover the joys of animal therapy

If you're struggling with how your relationship ended, are depressed, and lack motivation, it is easy to stay sedentary and rely on comfort food or alcohol to keep you numb. Push yourself to prioritize your physical and mental well-being. You will feel better in the long run.

Exercise helps to reduce stress and depression, increases the positive hormones in your brain, and keeps you physically fit.

A healthy diet can provide the nutrients your body needs to stay strong in trying times. Some may neglect to eat a balanced diet, and others may even go for long periods without eating. Poor eating habits while recovering from a painful experience will affect your mental health and productivity at work. If you don't eat well, your relationships with the people around you may suffer because you may not maintain the same mood or participate in the usual group activities.

Adequate sleep is essential for physical and mental health. Ideally, you can get at least six to eight hours of sleep each night. During sleep, your body repairs and regenerates tissues, and your brain processes and merges memories. When you don't get enough sleep, you may have difficulty concentrating, be more prone to mood swings and irritability, and be at an increased risk of developing many health problems, such as obesity, diabetes, and heart disease. To help ensure you get enough sleep, it's essential to establish a regular sleep routine, create a sleep-friendly environment, and avoid activities that can disrupt your sleep, such as using electronic devices before bedtime.

Make time for activities that help you relax and de-stress, such as art, hobbies, meditation, or spending time with loved ones. Having interests gives you something enjoyable to concentrate on and can strengthen your sense of self. You can channel your attention there and stop worrying about your previous relationships or stressors if you discover a new hobby.

You may already have interests you haven't had time to pursue while managing a dysfunctional relationship. Pick those back up again or find a new passion project.

Focus on the present moment and try to stay in touch with reality. By practicing self-care, you can better handle the challenges that may come your way.

Focus on Achieving Your Goals

Setting and working toward your important goals may be a helpful way to create a sense of purpose and direction in your life. Goals give you something to look forward to and a sense of accomplishment. Reaching your targets may help you feel more in control of your life, even after going through messy situations that you couldn't control.

Making new plans, a trip, or a new job may give you a new meaning and help you feel more satisfied with your life. Focusing on your goals and accomplishments can help you become more independent and empowered, which can be especially important after being in a controlling or unhealthy relationship.

Achieving your goals can provide a sense of pride and accomplishment, which can help you feel more positive about yourself and the future. It's important to remember that achieving your goals will not solve all of your problems, but it can be a helpful step toward building a happier and healthier future for yourself.

Find Someone Who Will Listen

The ability to move on after a breakup is aided by your support network. People need a healthy support system for situations like this, as they provide people you can turn to for comfort and advice. Consider joining a support group, either in person or online, where you can connect with others who may experience similar challenges. Sharing your experiences and hearing from others can be a helpful way to cope with relationship problems. There are also crisis hotlines for support and guidance.

Consider Working Elsewhere

If your environment at work violates your work boundaries or constantly fails to meet your needs, your peace of mind may be worth finding a job elsewhere. While it's difficult to make a change or not financially realistic, sometimes a completely fresh start can be the best thing you can do for yourself. Take some time to reflect on your current work environment, the specific challenges you are facing in setting boundaries there, and if some particular people or situations make it difficult for you to assert your limits.

You can explore your options by looking into other job opportunities or industries that might be a better fit. Consider company culture, workload, and growth and advancement opportunities.

Remember that changing jobs may take time and effort to find a new position that fits you well. Be prepared to do the work and be patient as you explore your options.

Moving To a New Location

I've met many individuals that found, after the end of an unhealthy relationship, they wanted a completely clean slate and a fresh start. While not realistic for everyone, deciding to move to a new home, city, state, or country allowed them to leave their unhappy past behind and make a literal fresh start elsewhere.

> A client of mine, Erica, once ended an engagement with a volatile alcoholic. She was devastated and had given him months to address his problems, but he would not make an effort. Crying, she called him from my office and told him to move out of their apartment. After several days of acclimating, she realized that they shared all the same friends, went to the same locales in their small town, and she would never be able to be free of his influence in her life.

> Erica took a month to look for jobs in her field, in cities she felt she would like to live in, and decided to move. She packed her bags and moved across the country to a new town, job, and fresh start, which was an excellent choice.

Of course, this is easier said than done when you are single, and you don't have children or a family depending on you. If this is a possibility and appeals to you, it can't hurt to look at your options.

You Are Stronger Than You Think

Discovering your inner strength can be a powerful and transformative experience. Think of it as a superpower that makes you overcome tough times. Leaving an unhealthy relationship can be a complex and overwhelming process. It is important to remember to trust yourself and the decision you are making for yourself and your new life.

> My cousin Sarah had been married to her husband, Jack, for ten years. They met in college and had always seemed to be a perfect match. However, Sarah felt something was missing in their relationship. They had grown apart and had different goals and priorities. Despite her reservations, Sarah tried to make things work for a long time. They went to couples therapy, but nothing seemed to change, and Sarah couldn't shake the feeling that she wasn't happy in the marriage.
>
> Eventually, Sarah made the tough decision to file for divorce. She knew it would be a tough road, but she also knew that it was the right decision for her. She couldn't continue living in a relationship that didn't fulfill her. The divorce process was complex and emotional, and Sarah had moments of doubt and sadness. But she surrounded herself with a robust support system of friends and family.
>
> As the dust settled and Sarah adjusted to her new life, she realized she could now focus on herself and her happiness and felt more fulfilled and at peace. While the road had been heart-wrenching, Sarah knew she had made the best decision for herself and was grateful for the opportunity to start a new life.

To be strong, you must reflect on your values, seek support, practice self-care, and focus on your future. Make time for activities that bring you joy, laughter, and fulfillment.

Conclusion

"Courage is going from failure to failure without losing enthusiasm." –Winston Churchill.

Be Optimistic and Smile

You've made some tough decisions. You are overcoming toxic and dysfunctional relationships, made the choice you deserve better, and are on the road to building the life you earned.

We covered how to identify toxic, dysfunctional relationships, what they may look like in your life, and how to recover from them. We've reviewed how to unlearn negative habits, create new, healthy behaviors, set new boundaries, and identify what type of life you want moving forward. The tips, strategies, and advice in this book arm you with what you need to thrive confidently after a dysfunctional marriage or a toxic relationship. You are well on your way to accomplishing your goals and should be incredibly proud of yourself and optimistic about your future.

When a random stranger smiles at you for no reason, smile back, a smile can be powerful- it tells your brain to be happy. That moment in space and time belongs to you, and it is a great feeling and one you can build upon in other areas of your life.

You deserve to feel fantastic about yourself, be proud of your accomplishments, and have others treat you respectfully. Everyone deserves to have a meaningful, loving relationship and sometimes it just takes a few tries to find it. You've taken the first step of realizing you need to make a change, and you've done it on your own. You are now on the road to healing by being willing to adjust your expectations and behaviors.

Congratulate yourself for taking a firm grip on your life and demanding better. I applaud you for going on this journey, and I appreciate you letting me be a part of it.

Thank you for reading this book and taking steps to achieve your personal goals. I hope you can successfully apply the suggestions and advice included here to your life as I have done to mine.

Many readers are unaware of how critical reviews are to an author or how difficult they are to come by after a book has been purchased. I would be so grateful if you could write a brief **review**.

You can also send me a direct message with thoughts, questions, or suggestions at: **www.creativeworksbooks.com**. I appreciate feedback and read all emails sent to me.

Thank you for your time helping new readers achieve their best selves.

Be sure to check out my other self-help books, workbooks, and coloring books for further exercises and relaxing personal growth tools.

Alexis

Scan here to review on Amazon

National Abuse Resources

United States National Domestic Violence Hotline
Hours: 24/7. Languages: English, Spanish and 200+ through interpretation service
800-799-7233

Canadian Abuse Resource:
https://www.domesticshelters.org/en-ca/domestic-abuse-help-in-canada

United Kingdom National Domestic Violence Hotline
0808 2000 247

Australian National Domestic Violence Hotline

https://www.respect.gov.au › services

Additional Resources

This book was written with a supplemental workbook in mind, to help reinforce and practice the skills taught here. It is called, *Leave That Junk Behind* by Alexis Carter.

The art therapy coloring books and workbooks I utilize and have found success with are:

Relax with Flowers, A Coloring Book for Adults

Relax with Animals, A Coloring Book for Adults

Relax with Mindfulness Meditations, A Coloring Book for Adults

Relax with Positive Affirmations for Women, A Coloring Book for Adults

You've Got This Girl, A Teen Girl's Self-Help Workbook for Self-Esteem, Confidence, and Loving Yourself

All of the above titles can be found on Amazon.

Author Bio

Alexis Carter has a master's degree in forensic psychology. Her expertise is in developing self-awareness, healthy relationship strategies, and recognizing negative patterns and self-esteem issues that can lead to unwanted dysfunction in relationships and personal and professional lives.

Alexis aims to arm men and women with practical strategies and techniques to understand ingrained behaviors, develop healthy relationships, create realistic perspectives and priorities, and manage challenges and traumas that can affect personal success.

She has created a library of self-help titles, workbooks, journals, and coloring books designed to address self-esteem, coping strategies, confidence building, stress management, and mindfulness.

When Alexis is not helping others, she is a busy single mom of twins and lives in California with her children.

You can find more of her books on Amazon by visiting: https://www.amazon.com/stores/Alexis-Carter/author/B0BNH9SB5M or by scanning this QR code:

References

Al Odhayani, A., Watson, W. J., & Watson, L. (2013). Behavioural consequences of child abuse. *Canadian Family Physician Medecin de Famille Canadien, 59*(8), 831–836. https://www.ncbi.nlm.nih.gov/pmc/articles/PMC3743691/

American Psychiatric Association. (2022). Diagnostic and statistical manual of mental disorders. *Diagnostic and Statistical Manual of Mental Disorders, Fifth Edition, Text Revision (DSM-5-TR), 5*(5). https://doi.org/10.1176/appi.books.9780890425787

Anderson, J. (2014). The impact of family structure on the health of children: Effects of divorce. *The Linacre Quarterly, 81*(4), 378–387. https://doi.org/10.1179/0024363914z.00000000087

Arzt, N. (2022, November 25). *What a narcissist does at the end of a relationship.* https://www.choosingtherapy.com/narcissist-end-of-relationship

Babauta, L. (2007). *25 killer actions to boost your self-confidence.* https://zenhabits.net/25-killer-actions-to-boost-your-self-confidence

Beck, M. (2020, June 19). *5 ways to reclaim your life after a breakup.* https://www.themuse.com/advice/5-ways-to-reclaim-your-life-after-a-breakup

Benson, K. (2021, December 8). *Criticism kills relationships: Why this habit is poisonous.* https://www.kylebenson.net/criticism-kills-relationships

BetterHelp Editorial Team. (2022, August 2). *How to move on from a relationship and start healing.*

https://www.betterhelp.com/advice/relations/how-to-move-on-from-a-relationship-and-start-healing

Bockarova, M. (2016). *4 ways to set and keep your personal boundaries.* Psychology Today. https://www.psychologytoday.com/us/blog/romantically-attached/201608/4-ways-set-and-keep-your-personal-boundaries

Brady, K. T., Haynes, L. F., Hartwell, K. J., & Killeen, T. K. (2013). Substance use disorders and anxiety: A treatment challenge for social workers. *Social Work in Public Health, 28*(3-4), 407–423. https://doi.org/10.1080/19371918.2013.774675

Buddy T. (2013). *Do you know the warning signs of domestic abuse?* Verywell Mind. https://www.verywellmind.com/signs-someone-is-being-abused-66535

Buffalmano, L. (2018, September 4). *11 types of toxic relationships.* https://thepowermoves.com/toxic-relationships

Crackylmag. (2021, June 3). *Signs of disrespect in your marriage.* https://crackylmag.com/relationships/signs-of-disrespect-in-your-marriage

Cuncic, A. (2022, April 28). *What is the illusion of choice?* Verywell Mind. https://www.verywellmind.com/what-is-the-illusion-of-choice-5224973

Daniels, C. (2022, April 8). *13 causes of toxic communication in relationships.* https://www.adornedheart.com/toxic-communication-in-relationships-2

Eatough, E. (2021, July 15). *How to set goals and achieve them: 10 strategies for success.* https://www.betterup.com/blog/how-to-set-goals-and-achieve-them

Enriquez-Geppert, S., Smit, D., Pimenta, M. G., and Arns, M. (2019). Neurofeedback as a treatment intervention in ADHD: Current evidence and practice. *Current Psychiatry Reports, 21*(6). https://doi.org/10.1007/s11920-019-1021-4

Espada, M. (2022, September 9). *How to set boundaries at work instead of quiet quitting.* https://time.com/6212149/how-to-set-boundaries-at-work-quiet-quitting

Feuerman, M. (2021, April 5). *6 steps to leave a toxic relationship.* Verywell Mind. https://www.verywellmind.com/how-to-leave-a-toxic-marriage-4091900

Gaspard, T. (2017, January 24). *10 things to try before giving up on your marriage.* https://www.gottman.com/blog/10-things-try-giving-marriage

Gillete, H. (2021, June 12). *7 tips for setting work boundaries in your 24/7 schedule.* https://psychcentral.com/blog/tips-for-setting-boundaries-at-work

Gjelten, E. A., & Editor, L. (n.d.). *What causes divorce? 8 common reasons marriages end.* https://www.divorcenet.com/resources/common-reasons-marriages-end.html

Hawkins, A. J., Willoughby, B. J., & Doherty, W. J. (2012). Reasons for divorce and openness to marital reconciliation. *Journal of Divorce & Remarriage, 53*(6), 453–463. https://doi.org/10.1080/10502556.2012.682898

Hogan, L. (2021, August 24). *How to recover after divorce.* https://www.webmd.com/balance/features/life-after-divorce

Holmes, K. (2019, May 1). *Why women need psychotherapy now, more than ever.* https://www.brighterdaycounselling.com.au/why-women-need-psychotherapy-now-more-than-ever

Jacobsen, J. (2022, January 20). *15 tips for breaking up with a psychopath.* https://www.marriage.com/advice/mental-health/end-relationship-psychopath/

Jones, E., Mackenzie, M. (2019, September 23). 24 *Signs you are in a toxic relationship and need to let go.* https://www.womenshealthmag.com/relationships/a19739065/signs-of-toxic-relationship/

Jordan, K. (2022, November 24). *Breaking up with a narcissist: 5 tips & what to expect.* https://www.choosingtherapy.com/breaking-up-with-a-narcissist/

Kennedy, T. (2018, November 12). *10 strategies to keep moving forward when feeling stuck.* https://www.lifehack.org/816187/moving-forward

Lamoreux, K. (2021, July 22). *Just make it stop! 10 steps to end a toxic relationship.* Psych Central. https://psychcentral.com/blog/steps-to-end-a-toxic-relationship

Lamothe, C. (2019, November 11). *38 signs of a toxic relationship and tips for fixing it.* Healthline. https://www.healthline.com/health/toxic-relationship

Lancer, D. (2016, February 28). *Self-Esteem makes successful relationships.* Psych Central. https://psychcentral.com/lib/self-esteem-makes-successful-relationships

Marín, R. A., Christensen, A., & Atkins, D. C. (2014). Infidelity and behavioral couple therapy: Relationship outcomes over 5 years following therapy. *Couple and Family Psychology: Research and Practice, 3*(1), 1–12. https://doi.org/10.1037/cfp0000012

Mason, M. (2022, February 23). *Divorce rates statistics and trends for 2022.* https://memphisdivorce.com/tennessee-divorce-law/divorce-rates-statistics-and-trends-for-2022/

Milton, J., & Stockhausen, R. (2021, June 10). *11 toxic signs there's no emotional intimacy in your marriage.* https://practicalintimacy.com/no-emotional-intimacy-in-marriage/

Mind. (2022, August). *Self-esteem.* https://www.mind.org.uk/information-support/types-of-mental-health-problems/self-esteem/about-self-esteem

Morin, A. (2019). *5 ways to start boosting your self-confidence today.* Verywell Mind. https://www.verywellmind.com/how-to-boost-your-self-confidence-4163098

Nguyen, J. (2020, December 1). *Post-Breakup regret is real: How to know if it was the right choice.* https://www.mindbodygreen.com/articles/how-to-know-if-breaking-up-was-right-decision

NHS. (2021, February 1). *Raising low self-esteem.* https://www.nhs.uk/mental-health/self-help/tips-and-support/raise-low-self-esteem

O'mara, L. (2016, October 15). *9 ways to set boundaries with difficult family members.* https://copebetter.com/9-ways-set-boundaries-difficult-family-members/

Pace, R. (2015, October 12). *How to fix and save a broken marriage: 15 ways.* https://www.marriage.com/advice/save-your-marriage/6-ways-to-successfully-fix-save-a-broken-marriage/

Pace, R. (2017, October 5). *How to recognize and deal with an abusive partner.* https://www.marriage.com/advice/domestic-violence-and-abuse/signs-of-physical-abuse/

Pace, R. (2022, January 11). *15 ways of how to end a relationship without regrets.* https://www.marriage.com/advice/relationship/how-to-end-relationship/

Patterson, E. (2019, March 29). *How drug addiction hurts relationships.* https://drugabuse.com/guide-for-families/addiction-hurts-relationships

Pereira, W. (2021). *Toxic people survival guide how to deal with difficult negative.* https://www.passeidireto.com/arquivo/102275662/toxic-people-survival-guide-how-to-deal-with-difficult-negative

Perry, E. (2022, August 25). *How to set boundaries at work: A personal guide to drawing the line.* https://www.betterup.com/blog/how-to-set-boundaries-at-work

Pietrangelo, A., & Raypole, C. (2022, January 28). *Emotional abuse: What it is and signs to watch for.* Healthline. https://www.healthline.com/health/signs-of-mental-abuse

Plumptre, E. (2021, November 17). *How witnessing domestic violence affects children.* Verywell Mind. https://www.verywellmind.com/the-impact-of-domestic-violence-on-children-5207940

Psychology Today Staff. (2019). *Therapy.* https://www.psychologytoday.com/us/basics/therapy

Reachout. (2019). *10 tips for improving your self-esteem.* https://au.reachout.com/articles/10-tips-for-improving-your-self-esteem

Scott, E. (2022, November 4). *What is a Toxic Relationship? How to Spot the Warning Signs of Toxic Relationships.* https://www.verywellmind.com/toxic-relationships/

Smith, S. (2021, May 17). *15 signs of a dysfunctional relationship.* https://www.marriage.com/advice/relationship/signs-of-a-dysfunctional-relationship/

Smith, S. (2022, February 3). *15 signs to know when enough is enough in a relationship.* https://www.marriage.com/advice/relationship/enough-is-enough-in-relationship/

Smith, S. (2022a, March 29). *10 toxic communication patterns that hurt relationships.* https://www.marriage.com/advice/communication/toxic-communication-patterns/

Stibich, M. (2018). *How bad relationships affect your health.* Verywell Mind. https://www.verywellmind.com/how-bad-relationships-affect-your-health-2223881

Stiles, M. M. (2002). Witnessing domestic violence: The effect on children. *American Family Physician, 66*(11), 2052–2067. https://www.aafp.org/pubs/afp/issues/2002/1201/p2052.html

Stockton, E. (2022, February 17). *6 ways drugs & alcohol can affect relationships.* https://rrtampa.com/6-ways-drugs-alcohol-affect-relationships/

Talbbl, R. (2017, August 16). *Managing your life in a dysfunctional relationship.* https://www.psychologytoday.com/us/blog/fixing-families/201708/managing-your-life-in-dysfunctional-relationship

Tracy, N. (2021, December 30). *Psychologically abusive relationships: Are you in one?* https://www.healthyplace.com/abuse/emotional-psychological-abuse/psychologically-abusive-relationships-are-you-in-one

Tsavoussis, A., Stawicki, S. P. A., Stoicea, N., & Papadimos, T. J. (2014). Child-Witnessed domestic violence and its adverse effects on brain development: A call for societal self-examination and awareness. *Frontiers in Public Health, 2*(178). https://doi.org/10.3389/fpubh.2014.00178

Tse, I. (2013, May 30). *5 ways relationships are bad for your health.* https://www.livescience.com/35469-5-ways-relationships-are-bad-for-your-health.html

Tzvi. (2016, July 26). *Four toxic patterns of communication in marriage.* https://aish.com/four-toxic-patterns-of-communication-in-marriage/

WebMD Editorial Contributors. (2022, December 16). *Signs of an emotionally abusive relationship.* https://www.webmd.com/sex-relationships/signs-emotionally-abusive-relationship

Women's Resource Center. (2018, April 12). *7 benefits of mental health counseling.* https://www.mywrc.org/mywrc/7-benefits-mental-health-counseling/